£3.49⁵⁴

C000103444

REAL MEN
DRINK
PORT
...and ladies do too!

REAL MEN DRINK PORT

...and ladies do too!

A contemporary guide by

BEN HOWKINS

Illustrated by Oliver Preston

FOREWORD BY HUGH JOHNSON

Quiller

Copyright © 2011 Ben Howkins
Illustrations copyright © 2011 Oliver Preston

First published in the UK in 2011
by Quiller, an imprint of Quiller Publishing Ltd

Distributed in the USA by: The Wine Appreciation Guild, South San Francisco CA 94080
www.wineappreciation.com

British Library Cataloguing-in-Publication Data
A catalogue record for this book
is available from the British Library

ISBN 978 1 84689 112 0

The right of Ben Howkins to be identified as the author of this work has been asserted in accordance with the Copyright, Design and Patent Act 1988

The information in this book is true and complete to the best of our knowledge. All recommendations are made without any guarantee on the part of the Publisher, who also disclaims any liability incurred in connection with the use of this data or specific details.

All rights reserved. No part of this book may be reproduced or transmitted in any form or by any means, electronic or mechanical including photocopying, recording or by any information storage and retrieval system, without permission from the Publisher in writing.

Book and jacket design by Sharyn Troughton
Printed in China

Quiller

An imprint of Quiller Publishing Ltd
Wykey House, Wykey, Shrewsbury, SY4 1JA
Tel: 01939 261616 Fax: 01939 261606
E-mail: info@quillerbooks.com
Website: www.countrybooksdirect.com

CONTENTS

DEDICATION

For Jamie, Annabelle, Ollie and Lucy

ACKNOWLEDGEMENTS

I AM DEEPLY INDEBTED TO Andrew Johnston and his splendidly cheerful team at Quiller for carrying out such an inspiring 'William Webb Ellis'. Elliott Mackey wanted to, but the recession got in the way.

And it all started with Hugh Johnson advising me to write a new book rather than revise another addition of 'Rich Rare & Red', as I knew all the 'Port people'.

The 2009 Belvoir Game Fair provided my first encounter with my hero, the brilliant cartoonist, Oliver Preston. Ollie's contribution completed my vision.

I particularly want to thank Lucy Howkins, having honed her skills at Bloomsbury and now at HarperCollins, for her loving encouragement and professional criticism.

Also, Clarissa, for seemingly not minding this prolonged, and sometimes tense, gestation period, and she still has not read the book. A loving thank you.

In Oporto I found wonderful cooperation from port's movers and shakers and would like to gratefully thank: Michael, James, Paul, Rupert, Johnny, Dominic and Charles Symington (phew !), Alistair Robertson, Huyshe Bower, Adrian Bridge, Robin, Elsa and Olga Reid, Johnny Graham, Jean and Johnny Hoelzer, Peter Cobb and Cristiano van Zeller.

In London, my similar thanks go to three Bs: Simon Berry, Hew Blair and Adam Brett-Smith.

In New York, renewed thanks to Michael Yurch and Peter Morrell.

Many wine trade friends, retired shooting friends and proper job friends have wittingly or unwittingly provided some wonderful material. Some of which is quoted unexpurgated. Some severely edited. Some simply OTT.

Thank you all so much.

Ben Howkins
Staverton
June 2011

FOREWORD

THE UNSPOKEN SUBTITLE OF BEN HOWKINS'S SECOND BOOK is 'Confessions of a Wine Merchant'. What he confesses is hardly likely to interest the public prosecutor, but it is going to strike a resounding chord in the sort of Englishman (he is unfashionably specific) he eloquently and lovingly describes and analyses in what amounts to a self-portrait.

Ben personifies the club-dwelling Port Person – except that he is a long way from the gout, the florid complexion and bulging waistcoat he almost invites you to imagine. His other natural milieu is the ski-slope. You won't find him stretched out in an armchair after lunch with *The Times* over his face. He'll be knocking on doors to find more converts to the good life he describes – a world of sharp corkscrews and sharper repartee.

Do you spot a contradiction? Yes, what spinach was to

Popeye, port is to Howkins… and it seems many of his friends. When you read his tales of those athletes of the port bottle, our eighteenth-century politicians and squires, the challenge is clear.

Ben's day job is no longer port. In the past twenty years he has steered what you might see as a rival enterprise, a wine even more ancient, sequestered and *sui generis*: Tokay.

The truth is that tokay reaches parts that port can't reach… and vice versa. Ergo Ben's double mission in life, his success and high spirits.

There's a model to follow.

Hugh Johnson

PREFACE

THE NOTORIOUS EIGHTEENTH-CENTURY SHROPSHIRE SQUIRE, John 'Mad Jack' Mytton, reputedly broached his first bottle of port whilst shaving. The bottles may have been pint-sized then, but four to six bottles a day?

William Pitt the Younger 'liked a glass of port very well and a bottle better'. Aged fourteen, he was prescribed a bottle of port a day by his doctor. He became Prime Minister aged twenty-four, a position he was to hold on to for twenty-three years.

Admiral Lord Nelson, Horatio to his friends, dipped a finger in his glass of port to draw a map for his basic tactics for the Battle of Trafalgar. How better to fortify oneself than with a fortified wine?

The Duke of Wellington enjoyed a glass of port before his famous victory at Waterloo. The exceptional 1815 vintage port has always been called 'Waterloo 1815' ever since.

These port people were all characters and all winners. History is layered, if not littered, with such colourful personae. There is something rather British, rather raffish, rather heroic about such stalwarts. They demonstrate our ability to laugh at ourselves; our love of continuity and yet our yearning for change; our qualities such as stoicism, mellowness and eccentricity.

A port person looks you straight in the eye: none of this glancing-over-the-shoulder business, trying to catch more important eyes. Few have this gift of making you feel that you are the only person that matters. Monsignor Gilbey, the renowned Catholic chaplain at Cambridge for thirty-three years, was one such port person.

So they are not social climbers. They feel comfortable in their own skins. Port people have a code of honour, a mischievous sense

of duty and an engaging sense of humour. Courage, tenacity and trust are their hallmarks. Shifty and mean they are not.

Adventurers and heroes were the original port people. Their daily intake both kept them warm and gave them warmth. Port instilled a beguiling virility that few other wines could match.

Today's port people are their natural successors. This book honours yesterday's port people and, deferring to *Debrett's*, is dedicated to Port People of Today, celebrating the British character as seen through a port glass.

1 DINNER AT THE FACTORY

PORT IS A SPLENDIDLY EVOCATIVE FOUR-LETTER WORD. The Portuguese call their port wine *vinho generoso*. Port's consumers are, by nature, generous in spirit. The enjoyment of port conveys an understanding of human nature second to none.

I love champagne, especially old champagne, but it is too lissom, too bubbly. It sets you up, but a follow-through is needed, even if it is a sublime Pol Roger or Laurent Perrier. I love burgundy, especially old burgundy, but it is too feminine, too seductive. It leaves you wanting more. Even though it is a fine Beaune Grèves Vigne de l'Enfant Jesus. I love claret, especially old claret, but as we know, thanks to Dr Johnson, it is 'for boys'. Having said that, on more than one occasion I have been very happy to have been considered a boy: think Lafite and Leovilles, Loudenne and Meaume.

There are other wonderfully seductive drinks which almost seem mandatory on certain occasions. Tokaji with *foie gras* any time, a Bloody Mary on Sunday mornings or a mid-morning manzanilla in the summer months. But port is for men. And, of course, being politically correct, or incorrect, for some women. Port needs foreplay, which any of the above can more than adequately provide, but port satisfies the inner soul. Champagne, burgundy or bordeaux all gladden the heart, but port fulfils.

The renowned nineteenth-century wine authority, George Saintsbury, put it slightly differently, but equally firmly. 'Port... is incomparable when good. It is not a wine-of-all-work like sherry. It has not the almost feminine grace and charm of claret; the transcendental qualities of burgundy and madeira; the immediate inspiration of champagne... But it strengthens while it gladdens as no other wine can do: and there is something about it which must have been created in pre-established harmony with the best English character.'

The noted wine writer Alec Waugh would claim: 'The year of vintage has no significance for madeira or sherry. It is for port that this particular distinction is reserved; and no wine fills a prouder and more honoured position at the English table. No wine is so truly English.'

He goes on 'The Englishman and his port'; what a world of Galsworthian tradition those five words evoke; of London clubs, and college common rooms and stately homes.

As the Portuguese proverb has it, 'all wine would be port if it could'. For three centuries, from the seventeenth century, port alone provided essential central heating for gentlemen; bespoke central heating at that. Winters were cold and long and houses were draughty and damp. At night, warmth may have been provided by ever-lovings, but during the day, corks had to be pulled to keep you warm.

Of course, periodic (or in fact pretty continuous) wars against France during this time favoured England's oldest trading ally, Portugal. Oliver Cromwell's Anglo–Portuguese Treaty of 1654 proclaimed that no Englishman in Portugal could be tried by a Portugese court. This put Englishmen above the law and so created a mini 'port rush' to Portugal. Port affectionately became known as 'the Englishman's wine'. It became the darling of the establishment. By the 1750s port had easily gained first place within Britain's drinking population. Light wines were on the way out whilst port's virility appealed to men with character.

These were exciting and restless times. Younger sons from vast, and not so vast, estates in both England and Scotland were encouraged to seek their fortunes abroad. France was usually bypassed because, as I said, we were usually at war. Beyond the tempestuous Bay of Biscay lay the colourful, encouraging coastline of Northern Portugal. These youthful adventurers had brought cloth to trade. They tasted the local wine, traded their cloth, and shipped this red wine back to Merrie Olde England. The Methuen Treaty of 1703 encouraged trade with Portugal and accelerated England's love affair with 'Red Portugal'. Additionally, the 1713 Treaty of Utrecht narrowly avoided giving France 'favoured nation' status, thus giving happy impetus to the embryonic port trade. At this stage, according to Charles Minoprio, the noted Master of Wine historian and wit, port was no more than *'ersatz claret'*.

It was duly sniffed, studied and sunk by gentlemen who knew how to enjoy themselves. Port became part of the proper Englishman's character, giving rise to the coveted term 'a Port Person'.

It could be said that the story of port began with two Englishmen, Mr Warre from Somerset and Mr Croft from Yorkshire. The port companies with which their names are forever associated were amongst the earliest, founded in 1670 and 1678 respectively. Both companies are still going strong today, more than three hundred years later.

King Charles II had just been restored to the throne of England. He was to marry Queen Catherine of Braganza, thus cementing even further the relationship between the two allies England and Portugal. (I have the feeling that Charles II was a port person; after all, he restored the monarchy. Whereas Charles I was not – he lost his head.)

William Warre, arriving in Oporto in 1729, became one of the leading members of the British community there. His grandson, Lieutenant General Sir William Warre, distinguished himself during the Peninsular War. Lord Wellington, as he then was, asked Warre in a letter, dated 18 March 1812, if he would have a pipe of port bottled for him, marked with his name and taken good care of until his return, as he wished to keep it as a '*bonne bouche*'. *Bonne bouche* for what, one may reasonably ask?

In 2011, Bill Warre, their direct descendant, lives happily in Wimbledon, London, and is definitely a port person. Ever mischievous, ever courteous, a twinkle in his eye, a glass in his hand, Bill exudes bonhomie.

John Croft wrote a famous treatise on the wines of Portugal in 1787. The subtitle was 'on the nature and use of wines imported into Great Britain as pertaining to Luxury and Diet'. Isn't that marvellous? Luxury and diet... The perfect combination. No need to worry ever again about the first, let alone the twenty-first, glass. Croft's son was created a baronet on the advice of the Duke of Wellington. This Sir John Croft married a Miss Amelia Warre. We might even have had a new double-barrelled port brand, Croft Warre or Warre Croft.

Many, many years later, in 1978, the fifth baronet, also Sir John, was extremely helpful when Croft were organising tercentenary celebrations for 'his' firm. We (I was a director at the time) buried a time capsule in Croft's lodges, complete with a copy of *The Times* and our export price list, to be opened exactly one hundred years later. I wonder which will cause the most excitement. The doyenne of wine writers, Jancis Robinson, had just started writing about wine a few years previously, and as she recounts in her *Confessions of a Wine Lover*, on the first night of the three-day celebrations, she was left to dine alone in her hotel. I am sure that never happened again.

As the current Duke of Wellington remarked at the time, 'I am sure the first Duke would have been happy to join the eighth in congratulating a great company on its tercentenary'.

The original Portuguese port person has to be the Marques de Pombal, formerly Sebastiao Jose de Carvalho and also the first Count of Oeiras. He was effectively King Joseph I's Prime Minister. Having swiftly dealt with Lisbon's massive 1755 earthquake, the following year he established a demarcated region for port production, thus creating a quality base for this embryonic world tipple. He also created a man-made port, as in harbour, in Leixoes, a few miles north of Oporto. The mouth of the River Douro had become so sanded up that few boats could get in or out safely. This new property development was essential for vital exploration and exports. Without his foresight and vision, the whole port enterprise might have been mired in uncertainty.

Another personality who should be mentioned is James Forrester, who arrived in Portugal to join his family firm, Offley Forrester, in 1831. He was a brilliant cartographer and engraver.

He was a purist, a linguist, charming, elegant and self-deprecating. He would certainly have looked all his friends in the eye, be they rich or poor, noblemen or farmers. He was created Barao (Baron) Forrester by the grateful Portuguese for all his significant contributions to agriculture.

Rory Forrester, a direct descendant, lives on the Isle of Mull in Scotland and co-hosts a cricket match each year. During frequent visits to Mull, I have been fortunate enough to have caught the selector's eye on a few occasions, and played for South Mull versus North Mull. In one memorable match in 2009, we played in wellington boots on a rain sodden pitch. As Rory's co-host said at the time, 'There are always reasons not to do things on Mull'. We were determined to play and so we did. Later that evening we did indeed celebrate, with Quinta do Noval 1985.

By contrast, the iron-willed Dona Antonia Ferreira, equally gifted, was not a port person. Not because she was a woman, I hasten to add. She was referred to as 'the Queen of the Douro'. She built schools, hospitals, roads and vineyards for her family firm, Ferreira. However, by all accounts, it seems she was deficient in the sense of humour department.

These two legends in their own lifetimes, a helpful prerequisite for gaining port-person status, are forever linked together in life and in death. Forrester and Ferreira were visiting the magnificent Quinta de Vesuvio by boat. The River Douro was in full spate, the rapids ever treacherous. Their flat-bottomed boat, a traditional *barco rabelo*, was thrown onto a rock at Cachao de Valeira. The Baron was drowned because he was wearing a money belt, heavy with coins, with which to pay his workers. The 'Queen' was saved by her crinoline. Both were heroes, but only one a real port person.

A much loved nineteenth-century port persona was Cabel Roope of former port-shippers Hunt Roope. Roope was once asked at the races by King Carlos I whether he had a horse in the next race. Roope replied in his excruciating Portuguese, 'Sir, *teno uma cavala muito beng* thought of' which actually meant 'Sir, I have a very well thought of mackerel', the Portuguese for horse being cavalo, not cavala!

Roope was a Victorian eccentric: seldom sober, he achieved little more than being loved by all. I think we all have a special friend like that. He once went to sleep on a train. At journey's end, miles from home, when he woke up again, he put out his boots for his butler, Sam Weller, as he always did at home. Another time, after lunching with the C-in-C of the channel fleet in Vigo Bay, when leaving the flagship he was confronted by a phalanx of naval ratings, similar to a sovereign's escort. Roope mistook them for a line of waiters at one of the grander hotels. Panicking, he asked his friend Max Graham if he would do the tipping...

Other port personae emerged over the years. George Sandeman became the one-hundredth Governor of the Bank of England in 1895. I wonder what he would have made of today's independence. His brother, Colonel Glas Sandeman, invented the penny-in-the-slot machine. It seems a long way from Brighton pier to the Bellagio in Las Vegas. Their manager in Oporto at the turn of the century gloried in the name of The Right Hon. Sir Spencer Cecil Brabazon Ponsonby-Fane, KCB.

I can vouch for the fact that at least two of the Sandeman direct descendants, George and Patrick, are both port people. Successful, jolly, self-deprecating and always having time to talk. Patrick tells me of the journalist who pestered his father, David Sandeman, about how long a bottle of vintage port would keep in a decanter once it had been decanted. Days maybe, weeks even? 'Absolutely no idea' was the immediate reply. When pressed further, and further, David explained patiently that he had never left a dining room table leaving a drop in the decanter, so the question was irrelevant.

R. J. Yeatman , of the Taylor Fladgate and Yeatman family, co-wrote the hilarious spoof of British history *1066 and All That* which became a musical comedy hit in 1938. The full subtitle was A Memorable History of England, comprising All the Parts You Can Remember Including One Hundred and Three Good Things, Five Bad Kings and Two Genuine Dates.

All these hardy and hearty port producers were the ultimate expats. They created their own oasis in a foreign country. Within this oasis, they created a set of rules and customs. They laid down a sense of belonging and a style of occasion that has endured to the present generation. The Factory House in Oporto embodies all these virtues. John Delaforce, of another long-established port family, has excellently chronicled the origins of this splendid granite outpost close to the River Douro in his book *The Factory House at Oporto*. His son David is an old colleague and friend with whom I have shared many port moments.

The Factory House, in the Rua Nova dos Ingleses (literally 'New English Street'), was an eighteenth-century creation where merchants and factors met for business. It was never a factory in the modern sense. This Palladian masterpiece was built between 1785 and 1790 by Consul John Whitehead, whose brother-in-law was William Warre, or, to give him his full title, Lieutenant-General Sir William Warre CB, KTS.

I will never forget the two-hundredth anniversary ball in 1990. I was co-hosting a dinner at Taylor's before the ball. My wife, who was due to fly out from London to join me, telephoned from Madrid to say that her plane had been diverted from Oporto and the airline had unceremoniously dumped her and a gang of ball-goers at Madrid airport in mid afternoon. Several people elected to return to England: not port people, on reflection. My wife and three friends hired a minute Fiat 500 and set off westwards across the desolate Spanish plain. They drove through John Wayne filmsets, over the rugged Spanish–Portuguese border and then

followed the winding River Douro to its Atlantic outpouring in Oporto.

Meanwhile, back in Oporto, after dinner, my guests went on to the ball. This was pre mobile phones. I calculated my wife's arrival time, assuming about eight hours' driving. I seated myself at a table outside Oporto's grandest hotel, the Infante de Sagres, on the pavement, in my dinner jacket. Armed with a bottle of

Taylor's 20-year-old tawny and a fat cigar, I waited and waited and waited. I had prepared hot baths and the obligatory gins and tonic. They arrived triumphantly at 1.30am. By 1.50am we were gliding down the hill to the Factory House. We entered just as Princess Alexandra, the guest of honour, was leaving. But honour was indeed satisfied.

Not only does the Factory House possess a wonderful ballroom, complete with chandeliers, in the Drawing Room there is always a copy, on display, of the London *Times* of exactly one hundred years ago. Now that is style. In fact there is a complete collection of *The Times* going back to 1788.

On one visit, in December 2010, I settled down to read *The Times* of 4 December 1910, exactly one hundred years ago. There was also an extract from *The Times* of 4 December 1810, 'His Majesty (King George III) continues the same as he was in the morning'. What an historical link to the present, and all in the same almost untouched room.

The paper was published at 4am and was number 39,448. Births were declared on the front page. There were the ads: The City of London Truss Society, for the relief of the poor throughout the Kingdom. Foxhunting on the bioscope... animated photographs. Disengaged household servants seeking jobs.

The headlines included: Labour troubles in France. Lord Kitchener in Egypt.

Political comments: Progress of the General Election with a printed swingometer. Mr Hearst's forthright views – 'The House of Commons is the entire government. The House of Lords has practically ceased to exist. The King is a sort of... appendix.'

Court circular: The Queen arrived from Sandringham to Buckingham Palace this evening.

Theatre: Cinderella is playing in the West End at the Playhouse.

Business: The stock market is 'idle with a dull tendency'.

Well, well, well. Has the earth moved or are we in a time warp?

The Writing Room has visitors' books going back to 1812. The current one dates back to 1944 when the Reids and the Symingtons dominate the first page. The Reading Room contains unique maps of the Peninsular War, showing how the English fought so hard to repel the French.

The valuable Library possesses over twenty thousand books, including many old and rare first editions. All books are accessible, not hidden behind some impenetrable wire. You can actually touch and read. (You can also, get this, smoke as you do so.)

Darwin's first edition of *On The Origins of Species*, written in 1859, lies on top of a table having recently been read at leisure. This is a grand, but informal library at its best. The first book that I pull out is titled *The Making of an Englishman* by W. L. George published in 1914. Chapter One, headed 'Rule Britannia', is dedicated to the small French boy who, in 1894, 'first called me John Bull'. Another book that catches my eye is *How to be Happily Married*. Chapters range from 'Cupid is blind', 'On making the best of a bad matrimonial bargain' to 'What is the use of a child?'. The chapter that seems way ahead of its time is called 'Nursing Fathers'.

The Old Kitchen sits pertly at the top of the building so as to keep its aromas away from the diners. However, the most memorable and wondrous part of the Factory House is the Dining Room or more accurately, the Dining Rooms. Dinner is served in one, port is taken in the other. After dinner is served around an elegant table seating forty-six you rise from your seat, and progress through the newly opened French doors into an adjacent and identical dining room next door. You take your place in exactly the same position as the one you have just left, and continue to enjoy your port and cigars. In the candlelight this is a time for reflection, conversation and contemplation. Nothing has really changed in two hundred years: and no one feels guilty. That is truly civilised.

The Factory House can appear to be a forbidding granite block when empty; but is a wonderfully welcoming home when full. The Queen and the Duke of Edinburgh were made welcome there in 1957. This happy occasion is recorded in gold letters on illuminated parchment. Prince Charles and Princess Diana visited in 1987.

Many years previously, Portuguese royalty had, somewhat unusually, also been welcomed to this most British of institutions: Queen Dona Maria II in 1834 and King Manuel II in 1908. Royal occasions are also captured by one of Portugal's greatest artists, known as Vieira Portuense. King Edward I and Queen Eleanor are portrayed in the well-known episode in which she sucks the poison from her husband's wound.

The freehold of this unique, extraordinary monument to the original port people was bought for £8 in 1848. The owners, since then, have remained constant. They are the British port producers who, as Members of the Factory Association, continue to own and administer this magnificent oasis within an oasis. Due to recent amalgamations of port producers, this means that there are currently only three member firms – Symingtons, Taylor's and Churchill's. It is these three thoroughly British firms, who control the vast majority of top quality port sales throughout the world, who also own Oporto's most enduring port edifice.

These port producers, splendidly relaxed expats, were not just creating a great international drink. They were creating a lifestyle, which they exported in equal measure. Port became a symbol of elegance, wealth and refinement. It was enjoyed, at length and at leisure, after luncheon and after dinner. It became one of life's great pleasures into which gentlemen could retreat.

The British, or rather it has to be the English here, as we never have had a British cricket team, also established a cricket club in 1855. This later merged with the Oporto British Club, to form the Oporto Cricket and Lawn Tennis Club. Cucumber sandwiches are still served at tea time; white port is on tap.

OPORTO CRICKET AND LAWN TENNIS CLUB
'... WHITE PORT IS ON TAP...'

Visiting teams have been a regular feature since the 1920s. Then, as now, representatives of the MCC, the Law Society and the Wine Trade were and are popular visitors. 'A gaggle of raffish Anglo-Portuguese friends were at the bar. We enjoyed a most civilised buffet for us five by the open fire in the dining-room ending with a 10-year-old tawny port'. The best things in life never change.

In the early part of the twentieth century the Portuguese royal family were eager to patronise and encourage all forms of sport in their kingdom. In 1902, King Dom Carlos and Queen Dona Amelia were present at the first football match between Lisbon and Oporto. The Queen arrived at half-time. Never having witnessed a football match, she had no idea what to expect. She became totally engrossed and intrigued by the antics of the players. At the final whistle she exclaimed that she had so enjoyed the 'second act' that she hoped the 'cast' would be willing to perform the 'first act' again. Is this the first ever request for an action replay, I wonder?

The celebrated historian Charles Sellers published his *Oporto Old and New* in 1899. This was followed up in 1965 by Gerald Cobb's *Oporto Older and Newer*. These books chronicle many of the poignant customs and sporting initiatives of the times. Shooting was mainly of red-leg partridges in the Douro. Cobb described it thus: 'Primitive country with guns lined down the mountainside between boulders.' Snipe abounded in the marshes near Aveiro and woodcock near Abrantes. The golf course at Espinho was founded in 1890, so was one of the earliest on the continent. The 'long hole', from the clubhouse to a finish through the front entrance of the neighbouring Cafe Chinez, became the basis of one of P. G. Wodehouse's short stories.

Back in England, port became the natural drink to accompany the Loyal Toast to the King or Queen: a product placement for which modern marketing men would give their eye-teeth.

King William II boosted the drink's patriotic image when he embargoed all shipments of French wine to England in 1693. As Jonathan Swift saw it in his poem 'On The Irish Club':

> 'Be sometimes to your country true,
> Have once the public good in view:
> Bravely despise champagne at court,
> And choose to dine at home with port.'

Incidentally King William IV, being a tall man, remained seated at sea during the Loyal Toast. This custom is an enduring protocol that sailors still adhere to in the Royal Navy.

The sea unites Portugal and England as no other two countries in Europe. Both are Atlantic Ocean countries, neither with a metaphorical foot in the Mediterranean Sea. This special relationship has endured over six hundred years of enviable political friendship.

James Woodforde confided in his *Diary of a Country Parson* on 3 April 1790, 'I drank but very little wine yesterday or today. Only two or three glasses. I used myself before, and all last winter, to near a pint of port every day... I now believe this did me much harm.' This did not prevent him recording on 26 December 1794, 'I drank plentiful of port wine after dinner, instead of one glass, drank seven or eight and it seems to do me much good, being better for it'.

Even doctors recommended port according to Woodforde: 'He

strongly recommends port wine and to drink more rather than less. She drank today between a pint and a quart without having the least effect upon the brain. She has not drunk less port for many days.'

Writers and artists have always seemed to enjoy their port and its attributes. James Boswell, Dr Johnson, Charles Dickens, Jonathan

Swift, G. K. Chesterton, Max Beerbohm and Toulouse Lautrec have all rhapsodised about port's qualities.

During their famous tour of the Highlands in 1773, those noted travellers Johnson and Boswell were heartily entertained at Lochbuie on the Isle of Mull. Boswell noted that in addition to being a delightful host, the Laird also kept 'admirable port', of which Boswell admits to drinking a whole bottle and suffering Johnson's reprimand the next day. The Laird, John, seventeenth laird of Lochbuie, was so honoured by this visit that he erected a stone plaque over the front door commemorating the visit: 'After leaving Moy Castle, the Lochbuie family resided in the house from 1752 to 1790 and it was in this house that Dr Johnson and Mr Boswell were entertained in 1773 by John Maclaine, XVII Laird of Lochbuie'.

I stand in awe of this plaque every time I visit Lochbuie. Oh to have been party to their conversation! But, by happy coincidence, we often enjoy breaking bread with Mr Boswell's descendants in Buckinghamshire. Sometimes, in my mind, I try to rekindle their ancestor's animated discourses of over two hundred years ago. Other times, 'midst the jollity that good friends induce, we just chat animatedly and pass the port.

Charles Dickens in *Nicholas Nickleby*, in 1838, has Nickleby asking his butler for, 'a magnum of the Double Diamond port to drink the health of Mr Linkinwater'. Why is it that whenever I hear the word 'magnum', I feel a party coming on? Anyway, Nickleby's butler remembers well the date when the pipe was laid down. This wonderful tradition of laying down or cellaring a pipe of vintage port for your son or godson at his christening was prevalent in the nineteenth century. After all, six hundred bottles would only last a bottle-a-day man just under two years. But more seriously, vintage port has always been produced to be at its optimum drinking window to coincide with coming of age at eighteen or twenty-one years. It is the perfect way to celebrate both the boy's and the wine's maturity. Provided, of course, that the father or godfather has not already been there first.

Nowadays we jibe about giving our son or godson one case of twelve bottles: how tragic is that? It is however still interesting to see which turns out the better, the port or the boy.

Many nineteenth-century sportsmen, such as Squire John Mytton and R. S. Surtees' Jorrocks, were dedicated 'portophiles'. Sport and port went hand in hand. A hip flask of port in the hunting field was *de rigueur*. After a great day's huntin', fishin' or shootin', these happily contented souls rode back to their manors, castles or country piles. Dinner would be served. Noisy, often rumbustious, conversation would ensue. Ladies would then be asked to leave the table so that they could powder their noses and gossip to their hearts' content. This was the signal for the port to be brought to the table and also indicated the end of the formal part of the dinner so that the servants could also leave the dining-room.

This enabled a subtle change of mood. Chairs were pushed back. Tight waistcoats undone. Cigars lit. The bottle or decanter of port had to be handed round the table by the guests themselves. No servants, no overhearing of gossip, but a bit of manual labour at table: the first real evidence of upper-class self service? Hence the 'passing of the port'. And clockwise? Most gentlemen were right-handed and it was easier to pick up the port in your right hand and pass it to your left. Simple as that really.

With host and guests alike relaxed, conversation was uninhibited. I bet these men looked each other in the eye. Loyalty and trust, the hallmarks of a great day's sport, spilled over into each other's contented bodies and minds. This is why, many, many years later, port is still called the 'conversational wine'.

A state of mind, pre-BlackBerry, when nothing, but nothing would interrupt men truly enjoying themselves and feeling the better for it. Imagine these scenes and enjoy them.

So-called Hunting Port, usually a full-bodied wood port, was still readily available until the 1960s. Our hunting squire, John Mytton, would have his last bottle of port in the billiard room. Bottles two to five would have been worked at steadily throughout the day, having taken the first while shaving, as you will remember. Mytton, whose ancestor apprehended the Duke of Buckingham for rebelling against King Richard III, was however no slouch potato. He kept thirty racehorses in training, became a Member of Parliament and a Master of Foxhounds. He was an excellent shot and a diligent farmer. He frequently quoted Latin and Greek to his friends. He once mischievously bid farewell to his dining guests and saw them into their carriage. He then immediately jumped on to his horse and galloped along a shortcut across his fields and held them to ransom, masquerading as a highwayman.

Because of, or in spite of, his continuous intake of port wine, this somewhat mad character always lived life to the full. He used to ride his horse up the front steps of his house and around the drawing room. To get rid of hiccoughs one night, he set fire to his nightshirt, apparently hoping to frighten them away. Twice married, he had several children and fitted all this and more into thirty-seven short years. Indeed one of his direct issue, Stephanie, used to be a neighbour of ours in Wandsworth. She seemed perfectly normal to me.

Somehow, this brings us onto politicians. I knew they would feature somewhere. I have already alluded to William Pitt the

Younger, arguably the ultimate consummate politician. He obviously was not cold in winter (port kept him warm) and was Prime Minister for twenty-three years. He always had a glass of port beside him in the House of Commons. He introduced income tax (one bottle too many that day?), but capped it at ten per cent (after a particularly good bottle?).

Pitt was the greatest orator in an age of great oratory, so admired by his early biographer, Lord Rosebery. He entered Parliament at twenty-one, became Chancellor of the Exchequer at

WILLIAM PITT 'LIKED A GLASS OF PORT VERY WELL AND A BOTTLE BETTER'

twenty-three and Prime Minister at twenty-four. His achievements, whether confronting that most unsavoury of conflicts, the French Revolution, at war with Napoleon, finding an answer to the Irish question, sorting out King George III or his enduring rivalry with top Whig Charles James Fox, were all pursued against a libatious background of, approximately and conservatively, seven thousand bottles of port.

The Whigs averred that Pitt died of port drinking. Imagine that as a cause of death today: how triumphant that would be. The Tories said that he died of a patriot's broken heart.

Pitt's port intake was not huge by the standards then. This was the time when the English clergy considered their cellars more than their churches; when a great Scottish patron stipulated only that the ministers whom he chose should be good natured in drink. This surely is the key: central heating, whether it emanates from the radiator or the bottle, should produce good natured argument.

Admittedly, we are told that Pitt and a friend consumed three or four bottles each in an inn one night. On another occasion, Pitt and two friends had a blunderbuss discharged at them for riding through a turnpike without payment. Makes a speeding fine rather tame doesn't it? But it was the oft used words 'getting through a great deal of wine' that amazed Lord Rosebery in 1891. 'What this meant is scarcely possible to compute.' Today, such a habit would be categorised by that unattractive phrase, 'binge drinking'.

Pitt famously established the right of the Prime Minister to ask ministers to resign. I wonder how he would have fared in an interview with Jeremy Paxman or John Humphrys. Perhaps they might have shared a bottle or even a glass or two, or perhaps not.

William Hague, when writing his biography of Pitt and doubtless taking in Rosebery's comments of over one hundred years ago, was astounded at the absolute consumption of Pitt and fellow politicians. 'Were they all drunk all the time?' he asked wine merchant supremo Simon Berry. Even allowing for smaller bottles, pint size rather than 75cl and lower strength, 15 to 16 per cent proof rather than today's standard 20 per cent, the answer has to be in the affirmative. Simon Berry I know to be a port person; if William Hague reads this, I hope he will nod happily. His sense of humour alone should qualify him to be included.

Port's heyday, in a way, was the eighteenth century. The politics of that era meant that our love/hate relationship with our nearest neighbour, France, was seriously tilted towards the second option. The drinking of port became a symbol of an Englishman's animosity towards everything French. Port's very richness and strength seemed superior to the thinner red wines from Bordeaux, while its very character seemingly suited the politician's long arguments, discussions and lifestyle as well as the needs of Generals just about to go into battle. Indeed, two nights before the battle of Waterloo, the Duke of Wellington was at the Duchess of Richmond's Ball in Brussels, which in itself shows some style. There, he received a dispatch from the Prince of Orange and was shocked by the description of the speed of Napoleon's advance. Quite when he consumed his glass of port is not absolutely clear, but the rest, as they say, is history.

Whig politicians of the late eighteenth century carried on the port drinking tradition in the clubs of St James's. Charles James Fox famously held court at Brooks's and was caricatured by Gillray with his beloved port, for example in 'Returning from Brooks's' (1784), with a bottle of port in his jacket pocket, summarising the mood of the times. Port and cigars went hand in

hand during these wonderfully decadent decades. Cigar stocks were often twice the value of liquor stocks at these clubs.

The sportsman's name for a fox when out hunting is still 'Charlie', some say named after this remarkable Whig. It is appropriate that the late comedian Jimmy Edwards, when Master of the Old Surrey and Burstow, was often to be seen out hunting with a bottle of port in one pocket of his hunt coat and a flask of whisky in the other.

One of Mr Christie's earliest wine sales, on 18 July 1815, featured eleven thousand bottles (almost a thousand cases) of the very finest old port, 'of which a considerable amount is warranted to have been from four to nearly eight years in bottle'. This came from Brooks's wine cellar, following a dissolution of partnership. A letter to *The Times* from T. G. Shaw noted in 1851 'Port as the only suited wine for John Bull and his climate... the wine is rendered so powerful, that none but Englishmen can drink it'. Cyril Ray, the noted twentieth-century wine scribe, summed this up nicely. 'The sunshine of the south, in concentrated form, is sent to chilly northerners, for whom it was confected. The Stuarts drank to the King over the water in claret. The Whig country squires showed loyalty to the Hanoverian line in port... and of course the Queen is an Hanoverian.'

Bertrand Russell recalls William Gladstone, when he was Prime Minister, coming to stay at Cambridge University. At dinner, when the ladies had retired, these two were left together. 'He made only one remark. "This is very good port they have given me, but why have they given it to me in a claret glass?" I did not know the answer and wished the earth would swallow me up. I have never again known the full agony of terror.' Such was the power of port.

Oxford and Cambridge were, and still are, wonderfully fertile training grounds for the great pleasures of life. Port was no exception. As *The Times* reported in 1798: '"To which university" said a lady, some time since, to the late sagacious Dr Warren, "should I send my son?" "Madam", replied he, "they drink, I believe, near the same quantity of port in each of them".' As Max Beerbohm noted 'Port... the milk of donhood'.

A favourite Oxford story is of the rude teetotal don. When all his guests were asked by the Provost to fill their glasses, this don replied, 'You know very well, Provost, that I would rather commit adultery than drink port'. The Provost replied: 'So would we all, my dear sir, so would we all, but since we cannot, let us take a glass of port.'

2 THE POWER OF ELEVEN

DURING THE COURSE OF TIME, port evolved from its original state as a pretty rough, unfortified red wine, 'Red Portugal', to something altogether more sophisticated. Pioneer port producers, ever in the pursuit of quality, ventured upstream into the desolate mountainous upper reaches of the Douro Valley where the conditions produced better grapes and hence better wine. Quality improved, but the long voyage to England did not suit the wine. It really did not travel well and it needed help. Grape brandy was added to the casks to stabilise and thus fortify the wine. Over generations, it was recognised that colourless grape brandy was better added at an earlier stage, to the must during fermentation, to retain the richness, and sweetness, of the fruit. Port, as we know it today, was born.

Gradually two styles of port emerged, wood port and vintage port. Wood port is aged in cask and then is immediately ready to drink when it is bottled. Vintage port is aged in cask for two years and then bottled, but absolutely, definitely, not ready to drink for several years.

Some years ago, Taylor's commissioned a splendidly bohemian Frenchman, Jean Lenoir, to investigate all the different smell sensations that occur in port. The smells or aromas or bouquets in wine that you sense provide about seventy per cent of what you will expect to taste.

Lenoir proved, through the research and analysis of compounds, that twelve aromas predominated in port. These are coffee, caramel, blackcurrant, cherry, oak, chocolate or cocoa, raspberry, walnut, plum, liquorice, vanilla and violet. Primary aromas emerge from young wines and give the sensation of chewing fresh grapes. An inexpensive wine, probably from the New World, and less than twelve months old, would do this. Secondary aromas will be evident in young wines that have the art and ability to age. Tertiary aromas occur when the wine loses its immediate fruit characteristics and evolves towards greater complexity.

Dig deeper and you find that the coffee, chocolate and cinnamon elements in port come from the grape brandy added to arrest fermentation and from the burnt staves which created the cask. Acetaldehyde produces the splendid nuttiness in aged tawny ports, while butanol produces the delightful strawberry and raspberry aromas. All I would add is that whenever I have given little phials containing these different aromas to friends, no one ever guesses their identities correctly. Aromas may be important foreplay, but actual drinking gives more satisfaction.

Wood ports include young ruby, tawny and white ports which are the staple diet of basic port drinkers. These, by law, now have to be a minimum of three years old. Each producer has evolved his or her own style and the different types can be found in supermarkets all over the world as well as at the back of bars.

Wood ports also include reserve and late bottled vintage ports, for those who want to move up a notch or two. These types spend longer in their oak casks, slumbering in the cool, blackened lodges in Vila Nova de Gaia. They therefore have more character than their younger siblings. The handpicked grapes will have come from older vines in better terroirs, and as a result offer a fuller, richer style which needs more time to be enjoyed and appreciated. In a way these are teasing wines: fully mature in their own right, but just beginning to demonstrate what the grapes in this dramatic terroir can really produce.

Their top offerings are 10-, 20-, 30- and 40-year old aged tawny ports. These sublime ports, the colour of sunsets, have slumbered silently for even longer. Their average age is either 10, 20, 30 or 40 years, not the minimum age. The art of producing them lies in skilful blending. The older they are, the less colour they have, as the oak casks absorb the skin colours of the grapes. Enjoyed chilled on a terrace in the Douro or at home watching television, these aged tawny ports are guaranteed to put a smile on the face of the imbiber. These are 'ports of today'.

Vintage ports are those which, by law, must be bottled within two years of the vintage. They represent the most rich and long-lasting ports. They will also mature for many years, but in bottle on their 'lees', which will form a sediment and therefore will need decanting. Vintage port is the ultimate labour of love. It is the pinnacle of the port-shippers' portfolio. The grapes will have been watched all spring, all summer, all autumn. Only when the mysterious forces of sun and rain have come together in exactly the right order can there be a 'vintage year'. This is only likely to happen three times in a decade. Vintage port is the port drinkers' Shangri-La.

Taylor's 1927, Croft 1963, Graham's 1966, Fonseca 1977 – all have left an indelible impression on me. Equally, I am happy to see that more and more shippers are now beginning to produce their own single quinta or single vineyard wines. If the sun and the rain and the stars and the moon have not come together as they ideally should, then the resulting wine from the top vineyards is still usually pretty good. For example, in a vintage year, Taylor's will use a majority of its top vineyard Vargellas in its Taylor's vintage port. If there is no Taylor's vintage port that year, then the grapes and wines from Vargellas have to go somewhere and the majority will end up in a bottle with a Quinta de Vargellas label on. These single vineyard wines will probably not need as much ageing as a full vintage port and so can be enjoyed after ten years or so. Less expensive, they offer a very good alternative. Perhaps to be considered as after supper ports rather than after dinner ones.

In a nutshell, the producer does all the hard work with the aged tawny ports and presents them to us, the consumer, when they are ready. We buy them when they are ready to drink, they do not change when they are in bottle, they have a stopper cork and no messy wax. To boot, once you have opened the bottle, you can happily leave it on the sideboard for days and months without it going off. Difficult, I admit, when it tastes so moreish, but I am told it can be done.

However, with vintage port, you and I have to decide when to open the bottle. We probably will get the drinking window right to the nearest five years, but may be nervous about it.

Should I wait for another few years? Do I need to decant it and how? Help... What happens if I get it wrong? I certainly can't admit that I don't know what to do. Frowning is not the best way to open a bottle of vintage port.

The thing to do is to take it from its horizontal position and stand it up for at least twenty-four hours. (Actually, you really do not have to do this. Many a time I have forgotten to bring one up from the cellar or I have changed my mind about which bottle to drink.) Then scrape the wax off the top of the bottle. Select your longest corkscrew, because vintage ports have the longest corks as they are likely to be in the bottle the longest of most wines. Before you insert said screw, choose your favourite decanter and have it standing nearby, ready to receive. Then, as an optional extra, find your decanting funnel. This will help in two ways. It should minimise any sediment entering the decanter and will enable the port to shimmer down the side of the decanter rather than cascading directly to its floor. It is a kindness to the wine. It shows respect.

Draw the cork and pour the vintage port in as above. Of course you can use candles and torches, but I prefer common sense. When you have poured most of the bottle into the decanter, you will see that there is a bit left in the shoulder. You should stop either when sediment bits appear or when the shoulder still has some left in it. The bottle was originally shaped for this purpose. It also means that you, the provider of this most precious of liquids, can then pour the next half glass or so into your favourite tasting glass and enjoy it. You need feel absolutely no guilt because it will have some sediment within it of course, and this would be totally unacceptable to your guests.

The training ground for vintage port enthusiasts has long been Oxford and Cambridge Universities. Their ancient colleges have always prided themselves on their vintage port stocks. The richer the college, the more port they can afford to lay down. Undergraduates almost swam in it. My own university education took place at Amherst College, Massachusetts, where no one under twenty-one was allowed to drink alcohol, though I do remember barrels of beer being rolled across the lawn. But no wine, and certainly no port. 'Port' in the United States then came from Gallo in California. In fact Gallo sold more 'Californian port' then than was produced in the whole of the Douro Valley. Times they have changed.

City Livery Companies, Lincoln's Inn and Officers' Messes carried on this education. All these, and others, understood the importance of laying down pipes – so called after the Portuguese *pipa* meaning cask or barrel – of port so that future generations could benefit from their foresight as they were, in turn, able to benefit from that of their predecessors. Vintage port was thus a key element in any scholar's education and an essential ingredient for the maintenance of the quality of life.

This point was highlighted by legendary publisher Marvin Shanken, who started the wine enthusiast's monthly bible, *Wine Spectator*. In his foreword to James Suckling's book *Vintage Port*, he says 'This sentiment has guided British port consumption for centuries and with the 1980s, an ever growing number of people in the United States and around the world have come to appreciate its appeal'.

Port became the stuff of legends. Decanters were, it seemed, created specifically to contain hallowed vintage ports. A classic port decanter has exactly the same measurement around its neck's circumference as its height. Use a napkin and prove it. Not many people believe that. Much money has been wagered on this totally irrelevant, but highly lucrative piece of information.

There is something about a decanter of port that puts a smile on the face of the guest and host alike. No other wine can command this beguiling feat. The guest, because he knows that he is in for a sustained treat: no measurement of glasses here, no butler to discriminate, no sommelier's eye to catch. No, this is for the duration. The host, meanwhile, is happy because the fruits of his cellaring are about to be unveiled and he looks forward to the adoration for his generosity. But first he knows that he has his guests in his power. He will ask them to guess the vintage. The balance of reality and expectation is all.

Port people know how to entertain and how to be entertained. They know how to laugh with friends and at themselves. Port became a way of life. It coursed through gentlemen's veins. All anticipated that precious moment at the end of a long day, when the port decanter was passed, and passed again around the dining-room table.

To settle any remaining doubts about the correct etiquette in the serving of vintage port, it is this. The host will have tasted the port before it is served. In fact he will most probably have had several tugs at the wine, perhaps offered it to a few friends, but be thoroughly satisfied with it. The decanter will sit in front of him. I say 'him', but of course it could be a 'her'. (I love raised eyebrows.)

It is the host's prerogative to offer a backhander to his principal guest, who would of course normally be a lady who would be placed on his right. He fills her glass, whilst she is giggling saying no, no, but actually meaning yes, yes. He would then fill his own glass and offer to fill the glass of the neighbour on his left. This is really a polite way of getting the thing moving and allows the host to flirt a little with his other neighbour. She will also say no, no, but mean yes, yes. The same procedure would apply if it was man to man, should the ladies have already moved next door.

H. M. Bateman captured all this so well with his cartoon of 1924, 'The man who passed the port the wrong way'. It depicts the young blade who upset all his fellow diners through his ignorance of port etiquette and passed the decanter to the right... result, complete social ostracism. The modern day equivalent of shooting in a baseball cap, perhaps.

I, myself, have a pretty drastic solution to gain everyone's attention. My 1820s Sheffield silver-plated decanter trolley is pulled along the table on its silver wheels with two port decanters on board. It rides roughshod through plates, glasses, candlesticks, but rather like a rush-hour bus, gets through eventually. The advantage of this wondrous machine is that you can offer a choice and we all know that we are more likely to partake of a choice than a single offer. The best combination is a chilled 10- or 20-year-old aged tawny port in the front which guests can use as mouthwash – expensive mouthwash, but what the hell. This is the countdown to gentle hedonism. The vintage port sits behind, so that guests, and host, can then indulge in the proper stuff and linger on and on.

Inevitably, conversation between port people is so vivid and compelling that, on occasions, the decanter stands its ground and is not passed to the expectant recipient on the left. Some artful soul invented the Hoggett decanter, which, with its round base, could not be placed on the table, but had to be passed from hand to hand until it found its resting place in a specially shaped wooden stand.

A well-known 'bottle stopper', the Bishop of Norwich, gave his name unwittingly to the traditional cry of the man with the empty glass: 'Do you know the Bishop of Norwich?' The guilty 'bottle stopper' immediately apologises profusely and passes the port on. A variation on this theme is 'Do you know Jones of the sixtieth?' The answer of course is no, because no one has the foggiest idea of who Jones was in the first place. The questioner looks plaintively and longingly at the decanter amid much spluttering, much ribaldry and much communal fun. Can any other wine command such 'looking in the eyes' between friends? Eyes that exude such trust and loyalty?

The enjoyment of port is inclusive. You are drawn to an inner circle of friends. But if someone is excluded, then retribution can take place. The story is told of two brothers who were refused a glass of port one evening by their father. Furious and unforgiving, they hatched a plot. A seal had just been washed up on the sands

outside the house. They heaved it through the front door, past the gales of laughter being exhaled from the dining-room and up the stairs to their father's bedroom. Straight into bed it went, between the sheets. A pair of spectacles, *The Times*, and all was set. Father was not amused. The two brothers had to wait a very long time before they were ever offered a glass of port again.

It is good to have old friends, old friends and allies whom you can trust through thick and thin. Portugal and England have been allies since Henry the Navigator's Treaty of Windsor in 1373. It was three hundred years after this historic treaty that the first Englishman and Scotsman traded in port wine. No one then could have foreseen that the red grapes, not yet planted, in the upper reaches of the desolate Douro Valley, in some of the most inhospitable vinous terrain known to man, would eventually become the catalyst for a much envied lifestyle in some of the most civilised parts of the world.

For generations, Englishman after Englishman and Scot after Scot had trodden the same path, often literally. The journey from the Atlantic coast to the best vineyard sites in the Upper Douro, near the frontier with Spain, took three days. All rode west, upstream; the wine was then brought down by boat, downstream. This was not in an ordinary sailing boat, but as I have mentioned, in the unique *barco rabelo*, literally meaning the boat with the tail. Before it was dammed in the mid-1970s, the River Douro, festooned with rocks and rapids, was one of the most treacherous rivers in Europe. Rising in Spain and flowing neatly into the Atlantic, the passage amongst the vineyards was often so shallow that the only way to steer the flat-bottomed boat was to have a very long, low rudder that could balance the prow of the boat. The original clinker-built Viking boats had been sailed to the Mediterranean in the ninth century. Over the centuries these were adapted to navigate the River Douro.

In a typical spirit of comradeship, just before the hydro-electric dams enabled the river levels to rise thirty metres in the 1970s, Croft and Cockburn directors joined forces to experience the original downstream journey, with forty pipes of port. Croft was represented by George Robertson and Robin Reid; Cockburn by John Smithes and Felix Vigne. It is believed that these gallant directors were the first members of the British community in

Oporto ever to have joined their Portuguese workers in this annual water obstacle race. They experienced rugged scenery, sheer granite mountains on both right and left; shooting rapids and white-knuckle manoeuvres to avoid the whirlpools ahead. All the while the boat was carrying the equivalent of 2,400 cases of precious port to its maturing cellars.

This brave annual journey, carrying the new wine downstream, is now commemorated in May each year, by an armada of gaily decorated *barcos rabelos* racing between points at the mouth of the River Douro. But this is a mere amateur jog compared to the professional marathons of yesteryear.

Back then, the resilient English and Scots persevered. The schistous rocky soil, home to port's grapes, was well matched by their own grit. It was here, in the desolate majesty of the Upper Douro Valley, that they found their holy grail.

The farming cycle began with the blasting of the deep schistous rock with dynamite. Then followed the spring planting of the young vines on the incredibly steep slopes. After a wait of three years the first pickable grapes would appear. Surviving burning sun in the summer, sometimes snow in the winter, these grapes would eventually present themselves for picking by hand in September. Dozens upon dozens of local pickers traipsed mile upon mile to join the festive celebrations. Up and down the dry stone terraces, wooden baskets on their heads, the harvest was gathered in, from dawn until dusk.

Over time, the growers appreciated that some vineyards produced better wines than others. Different terroirs produced different characteristics in the grapes. This was the beginning of each port firm developing its own 'house' style, depending on where they sourced their grapes. For example, Dow ports are on the light, cedar-wood style, Croft ports are fragrant and also on the light side, whereas Graham ports are rich and powerful and Cockburn ports are deep and structured. These house styles were predicated from the beginning by their original vineyard microclimates. These would be due to different elevations, different varietals, different soil types and the adjoining vegetation.

The strength and character of different soils determines the quality levels of each vine and its grapes. Three of these four revered port names were Scottish in origin. The fourth, Croft, was originally from Yorkshire. No terrain in Europe more reflected the hardy island northern character more determinedly than the hardy, schistous rocky soils that determine the desolation of the Upper Douro valley. This was Scottishness at its best: searching for quality, higher ideals always in sight and enormous pluck in adversity.

To return to the production process: the gathered grapes would then be tipped into *lagares*, or stone troughs. Treading would begin. Arms linked, the happy treaders would plough back and forth in time to an accordion. The local marc, *bagaceira*, would lead them on and keep their spirits up.

Drawn into oak casks, this 'Red Portugal' stayed the winter

amongst the vines. The following spring, these casks or pipes were transported downstream to the port shippers' lodges in Vila Nova de Gaia, the town opposite Oporto. Here they would slumber silently, only being interrupted by the drawing-off of samples so that the quality control experts could determine how they were developing. Any complaints were immediately sorted out, the appropriate medicine was given. The happy port carried on sleeping. Much of the same could be said, for much of the time, about its happy owners.

The expat British community used to drive to their offices across the bridge, south of the river, to their 'factories' in Vila Nova de Gaia – so much more pleasing than driving to Gaia New Town. The morning post would be opened, swiftly followed by the bottles of port that needed attending to: straight into the tasting room (always best facing north, to catch the best light) to evaluate their little earners. Lunch was an important part of the daily routine. This was either taken in the dining room in their own lodges or with a friendly competitor. Once a week, on Wednesdays, they would cross the bridge again and all lunch together in the Factory House. There they would sign a few letters on their return to their offices, take a leisurely glass at the Oporto Cricket and Lawn Tennis club and then dine at home or with other port friends.

Much the same pattern continues to this day. The difference, though, is that emails and marketing have meant that these same owners have to work a hundred times harder than their forbears to maintain the same lifestyle.

A Bill of Lading book that I have in my possession illustrates this difference perfectly. In the same month that the Duke of Wellington was celebrating his victory over Napoleon at Waterloo, the entry in Croft's Bill of Lading book shows that one hundred pipes (6,000 cases) of port were loaded onto the good ship *Fly*, bound for London with or without convoy. These were to be delivered in good order and well conditioned. 'And so God send the good ship to her desired port in safety. Amen.' Once the vessel had reached her desired port of safety, the port shippers' work was done.

Nearly two hundred years later, the port shipper will be zigzagging his way across the world, flight after flight, creating demand for his brand and then satisfying this demand with promotional advertising and consumer offers. All this whilst wallowing in emails and meetings. Choice, progress? The fast lane seeking the slow lane.

Life in the Factory House, the Cricket Club, the family quintas up river and homes in Oporto mirrored life at St James's clubs, the MCC, country or town houses in England. It was this close working relationship between the two Atlantic seafaring nations that added to the indisputable fact that although the English did not invent wine, they did invent the demand for great wine. We really can regard this as a great invention in itself.

As my family will attest, I enjoy synergising numbers. Port's favoured number is clearly eleven. At its most straightforward this is represented by the anguished cry of the thirsty port shipper:

> 'I must have one at eleven,
> It is a duty that must be done,
> If I don't have one at eleven,
> Then I must have eleven at one.'

This catchy ditty, originating from Freddie Cockburn of the famous port family, echoes the belief that port shippers could not wait until the sun was over the yardarm at 6pm as in most other expat countries. 'Elevenses' was port. A later colleague instituted 'ten-ses', but only on dramatic, 'needs must' occasions.

Cricket is the game that epitomises the expats' favourite type of sport. It is leisurely, it is unhurried, it is a team game, it can only be completely understood by the English. It actually includes a tea break: an official tea break. And how many players are there in a team? Exactly.

THE POWER
OF ELEVEN

By contrast there are also eleven players per side actually on the pitch at any one time in American football. But here's the difference – no tea break.

During a hunting day, on arrival of the hounds at 11am, a stirrup cup is customarily offered to all those on horseback and to those who will follow on foot. Port has been this traditional stirrup cup, served as the welcome drink, for generations.

Incidentally, when *Brideshead Revisited* was being filmed at Castle Howard in the 1970s, an enterprising friend of ours positioned herself and her horse very close to the grand steps down which Anthony Andrews, as Sebastian Flyte, would descend to partake of his stirrup cup. This scene needed eleven takes so our friend allowed herself to enjoy eleven glasses of port. I do not think the horse was allowed eleven polo mints.

In England, King Henry VIII's second wife, Anne Boleyn, had eleven fingers. She was beheaded for adultery, incest and treason. I wonder what that tells us?

London had eleven postal collections per day in 1900. I know what that tells us.

In the United States, Franklin D. Roosevelt was related to eleven other Presidents, five by blood and six by marriage.

Historically, it was Rorke's Drift in Natal, South Africa, that arguably saw this magic number at its most elevated. Eleven VCs were awarded, the highest number ever in a single action, to the gallant British soldiers who defeated the attacking Zulus on that fateful day in January 1879. These brave men, all 104 of them, fought off 4,500 foot stamping, chanting Zulus, memorably recorded in the film *Zulu*, starring Michael Caine amongst others. The late David Rattray was able to bring this incredible battle so much to life, before his own life was so tragically shortened. Sitting on rows of hard chairs on this desolate hillside, at the precise time that the battle began, was a spellbinding experience. David was a master storyteller and I am told enjoyed his port. To a man and a woman we were moved to uncontrollable emotion as he unfolded the tale of this military drama against the setting sun.

But let's return to Portugal. The vitally important Methuen Treaty of 1703 comprises numbers adding up to eleven: add one, seven and three together. (This treaty was also known as the Port wine Treaty.)

The Peninsular War is never far from the port shipper's sense of history. The recapture of Oporto in 1809 heralded a fascinating role reversal. Instead of the defeated Marshal Soult, leader of the French army, enjoying the dinner that had been prepared for him at the Factory House that night, the victorious Duke of Wellington ate it instead. A century later, the fearless Cabel Roope organised a great centenary feast to celebrate that victory, and more importantly, the re-opening of the Factory House on 11 November 1811. (It had been closed for two years by the original invasion of Oporto by Soult.)

Roope discovered eleven descendants of the very port shippers who had been present at the re-opening in 1811. Percy Croft was one of these descendants. Percy's main claim to fame was his mantra 'any time not drinking port is a waste of time'. The eleven descendants met at 11am on 11 November 1911. They chose eleven dishes, eleven different wines and were served by eleven different waiters. The menu included lamprey, suckling pig and caviar. The wines included a Borges 1820 vintage port. Strange that this highlight came from a Portuguese shipper, rather than an English one: perhaps they could not decide which English one should be so honoured.

At the time of writing, plans are well advanced for another celebration, two hundred years on, for 11 November 2011.

THE RECAPTURE OF OPORTO
11TH NOVEMBER 1811

Port people certainly know how to entertain and how to be entertained. They know how to laugh with friends and at themselves. If the host asks his guests to guess the vintage, it is always advisable to go 'older' rather than' younger', believe me.

Fictional characters love their port, too. Dorothy L. Sayers's Lord Peter Wimsey was partial to Dow's 1908. P. G. Wodehouse's Bertie Wooster would have been lost without his post-prandial glass of port at the Drones Club.

As Daniel Rogov, an Israeli wine lover, puts it 'port's image...

nothing so completely English as the lord of the manor, in his oak-panelled library after dinner, sipping glasses of old port wine with good cigars…, and walnuts…'

I have a splendid book by my side written in 1926 by William Todd. He devotes a full ninety pages to the 'Buying, serving, storing and drinking port'. At the back of the book there is a reproduction of a handwritten pull-out graph entitled 'Curves of port imports to the UK, plotted for every decade from 1678–1923'. Seemingly, as a result of the 1914–1916 Anglo Portuguese Agreement, Todd forecast that port imports to the UK alone would pass the 100,000 pipes mark (6,000,000 cases) very quickly. Port was indeed The Englishman's Wine.

World War II, of course, changed everybody and everything. The regimented, but respected 'upstairs, downstairs' culture evolved into a climate of austerity and the true self-service era was born.

Port did not have a good war. In the event, a record 117,000 pipes (7,000,000 cases) were shipped to the UK in 1919, whilst only 35,000 pipes (just over 2,000,000 cases) were shipped to the UK in 1946. Clearly port consumption had changed irrevocably during the period between the wars.

Certainly the four to six bottles a day man had become extinct. Well, those who indulged on a regular basis anyway. Better clothing, warmer houses, electric fires, gas heating, the luxury of enclosed motor cars, all contributed to the slump in demand. The main cause was that dangerous word, choice. Choice, not in the grand dining rooms, the panelled libraries, the gaming tables of club-land, but in the Dog and Duck, the Red Lion, the Countryman's Arms; yes, in the pub.

The missus's port 'n' lemonade, as much a public bar fixture as the man's pint of bitter, became the target for drinks marketeers. Babycham wooed and won. Gently followed by Snowballs, Baileys and, now the clear victor, the ubiquitous Chardonnay.

By 1963, France had overtaken the UK as the world's largest port-consuming country, a position it holds to this day. Apart from the British, the Scandinavians have always enjoyed port. It keeps them warm, so, not surprisingly, they prefer more full-bodied, heavier wines.

A not so delightful, but amusing, apocryphal story is told about a lodge worker in Vila Nova de Gaia who accidentally fell into a large vat and drowned. Under the fully understandable rationale of not wanting to waste all that port, the producers tasted it and pronounced it absolutely fine. It was shipped in bulk to Scandinavia and bottled on arrival. It proved rather successful. The importers asked for another sample of the delicious 'full-bodied' port that they had received last time... a request that could not be fulfilled.

To overcome the overall decline in port sales, the shippers became more proactive in the dressing of their bottles. They started to understand the mood of brands better: they had to. From 1912, the then largest port shipper in the UK, Gilbey's, had promoted their 'Invalid' port brand, with 'medically good for your health' writ large on the label. It was targeted to suit the needs of invalids and convalescents but would at the same time 'be palatable for those fortunate enough to need no medicine'. In 1950, Gilbey's were banned by the Ministry of Agriculture from using this label. Overnight 250,000 cases went down the Swanee. The new brand name, 'Triple Crown', just did not have the same appeal.

Various members of this illustrious family are still involved in the wine trade. Tom Gilbey, even though he now lives in Scotland, is always happy to share a glass of port, though Triple Crown is not usually in his drinks cabinet.

Early advertisements such as 'Dare you tell your wife about Ruby?', Cockburn's 'Don't say Cock say Co' and Sandeman's 'The Don' were brave but simple attempts to arouse consumer interest. Other marketing ploys included one by Kopke, a port shipper of Dutch origin, who launched 'Bridge Port' for ladies who played bridge on verandahs in the Douro. Dow introduced 'Dark Club', which soon became a favourite in the Vatican apparently. Dow also followed up with 'Midnight Port', presumably more of a favourite in nightclubs or on the sofa, than with the Cardinals. Warre's tried to capture the imagination with 'Otima', with great success.

Not to be outdone by Dow, Delaforce's 'His Eminence's Choice' featured said Cardinals on the label and their 'Curious and Ancient' label was indeed curious and ancient, as was the delicious 30-year-old tawny inside the bottle. Graham's still has 'Six Grapes', which translates easily across the Continents as demonstrated by it being served on both the maiden voyages of the liners *Queen Mary* in May 1936 and *Queen Mary 2* in January 2004. Meanwhile, real mood names such as 'Hunting' and 'Invalid' remain strictly off-limits.

3 QUINTA-SSENTIAL ENGLISHMEN

My first visit to the Douro was in 1963, the year of a much-celebrated vintage.

On arrival at Cockburn's Quinta at Tua I was greeted by Reggie Cobb, whose first words to me after the four-hour train journey into the furthest reaches of port's demarcated region, were 'Come in, come in. I was at school with your father.' He went on to say: 'You must meet John Smithies of Cockburn's. He can spit and hit the ear of a dog at twenty paces.' I did and he could.

Robin Reid welcomed me to Croft's Quinta da Roeda by recounting how the formidable television chef duo, Johnny and Fanny Craddock, had recently been staying at Roeda. They had arrived in their enormous Rolls Royce. On alighting, Fanny had advanced towards Robin, her equally enormous bosom leading her majestically forward. Robin was transfixed. 'What's the matter with you, boy? Have you never seen tits before?' she demanded.

The English abroad: individual, friendly and funny. In Oporto and the Douro, they have not only survived, but have flourished happily into the twenty-first century. Still there are characters who continue their predecessors' wacky fortitude. As someone once said, 'Where there is the vine, there is civilisation'. Where there is a port vine, there is civilised conversation and plenty of wit.

This was the time of the Beatles, the Cold War, JFK's assassination and dodgy food in England. I was far removed from all this. Aged only twenty, against all the odds I had been awarded the annual Vintner's Scholarship. This coveted award from the Worshipful Company of Vintners enabled me to spend six months visiting the great vineyards of Europe. I started in Champagne, cruised southwards through Burgundy, turned left to Alsace, took in the Rhone, scampered through Spain down to Jerez de la Frontera and then onwards and upwards to Oporto.

Oporto itself displayed an incongruous mix of dramatic blue *azulejo* tiles and laundry hanging out to dry, both vying for attention on the sides of centuries old buildings. The streets were cobbled, busy and polluted. Trams ruled OK. I took refuge in the old British Club, in which we were too often too enthusiastic about our billiards games and too many balls seemed to exit through the large first floor windows. This was much to the consternation of the local constabulary, who were not really used to large, solid balls landing at their large, solid feet.

Live-in maids were the norm. Dinner was always four courses, soup, fish, meat and pudding and I am sure cheese came in somewhere as well. The descendants of the great port houses still partied together, entertained each other generously and were friendly rivals.

Every Wednesday, as now, all port shippers and their guests may lunch at the Factory House. At 12.30 they would leave their, often adjacent, offices in their port lodges in Vila Nova de Gaia and then traverse M. Eiffel's bridge and park their cars, somewhat haphazardly, around the Factory House. Greeted by the ever loyal Portuguese butler, these bastions of the expat community would chat animatedly as they ascended the cold granite staircase.

A quick look at *The Times* would reassure them that nothing much had really changed. A glass or two of chilled white port would kick-start their gastric juices as they ambled into luncheon. (I think the longer version of the word for midday meal is more appropriate in this context.) Luncheon over, they would eagerly lay their hands on the decanter containing old tawny port. This splendid liquid was often matured inland in the Douro country, rather than in their cooler, sea-coast lodges in Vila Nova de Gaia, to attain the fabled 'Douro burn' that the searing summer heat bestows on it. Rather deprecatingly, tawny was always referred to as 'mouthwash'. Then swiftly on to the many and several decanters of vintage port that festooned the dining table.

'I think this one's yours', one early imbiber might venture, eyeing one of his competitors knowingly. Competitor, cousin, confidante, each was treated in the same way. It was the winning that counted. 'This is Dick's, isn't it?' Always the individual, seldom the shipper. This was the inside track, not insider knowledge, but each participant part of an almost mystical brethren: each proud, each competitive, each individual. Each coaxing and teasing each other, eyeballing each other, pondering the many different taste sensations as they swirled the vintage port in their glasses. Which terroir did it remind them of? Which house style predominated? Was it their own? Which weather patterns could they recall? Did they like it? This naughty schoolboy game gave them immense pleasure. They could return to their offices across the river replete, happy. If they had guessed the vintage and the producer correctly that afternoon, that would have given them more satisfaction than if they had won the Derby or landed a big contract.

If life in Oporto might be compared to gently moving from one's office in the City to one's St James's club for lunch, then life in the rugged, desolate Douro was more like driving around one's estate in the Highlands of Scotland during the day and coming home for a well-earned supper in the evening.

Port shippers' quintas or wine estates were usually miles from the nearest town or village. They were built architecturally like tea planters' bungalows or local farmhouses. They had to be self-sufficient. The live-in domestic family lived there most of the year as if it was their own. When the port producing owner galloped or drove into sight, the proverbial suckling pig was prepared and the hospitality started afresh.

One of the duties of the port owner, whilst visiting outlying quintas from which he wished to buy the farmer's grapes, was to check the impressive wooden vats. *Si senhor*, oh yes, sir, of course they are clean to receive this year's wine. Robin Reid of Croft's opened one vat after such an assurance and a myriad of squawking chickens leapt into the air.

Vintage time in the Douro in the 1960s was rather like harvest time in England. The pessimistic farmer has somehow always attracted an array of support. Fergusons and stooks rather than combine harvesters and bales. Everyone wants to join in. When to pick? Can we get it in before the rain?

The English port shippers always used to decamp for a month or two up the Douro at this time. Some welcomed wives; others, such as Cockburn, treated the whole exercise as men only. The port shipper was the undisputed squire or laird of his territory. He, never she, would have many loyal peasant workers scampering to obey his orders.

The workers would bring in their friends and cousins to help pick the grapes during harvest time. It was hard work toiling in the often boiling sun, climbing up and through the terraced rows. The grapes would then be emptied into the *lagares*. These granite stone troughs held around 2,000 gallons of grapes in their raw state waiting to be turned into wine.

This happened, and still does, through treading. Even today there is a strong line of visiting city gents and county gentry who seem very eager to strip down to their M&S shorts and plunge their innocent legs into the sensual, viscous red juice that is halfway between the grape and the wine proper. Taylor's, Fonseca, Graham's, Dow, Croft and other great names still invite the select few to partake in this initiation ritual. They put their arms around each other's shoulders in a brotherly kind of way and march up and down for about four hours. Hay-making was never like this. Taylor's have some wonderful William Rushton cartoons depicting these scenes.

An accordion player keeps everyone in time. Local women take it in turns to enter this male workhouse in order to distract and dance. *Bagaceira*, the local grappa, is consumed in vast quantities once one's four hours are up. And yes, there are strategically placed holes in the wall for the relief of the bladder.

Invitations from famous port shippers were much coveted and eagerly sought after, both to experience the unique style of life enjoyed in the Douro and to meet its characters. George Robertson, for example, could entertain for hours with his guitar.

Robin Reid was a maestro on the drums. Dinner at Quinta da Roeda was always a fun, fun evening with Elsa Reid slipping effortlessly between Portuguese and English, her remarks characteristically prefixed by *'O menina'*. We used to reckon that it took a transatlantic visitor a maximum of three hours to totally and fully relax. John Burnett, Robin's successor, often led us astray with the local brandy. Brandy is fine after port, whisky is a disaster.

The Symington clan, now owners of a galaxy of top names such as Graham's, Dow's and Warre, plus Smith Woodhouse, Quarles Harris, Gould Campbell and their top quinta, Vesuvio, used to entertain mainly at their family-owned Quinta dos Malvedos and Quinta do Bomfim. I have been friends with three generations of this highly articulate and close family. Twins Ron and John, Michael, James and Ian from the next generation and now Paul, Rupert, Dominic, Charles and Johnny, whilst other Syms wait in the wings. This happy and successful family company is a showcase business model for any family-owned company.

Alastair and Gilly Robertson entertained beautifully at their elegant Quinta de Vargellas. Huyshe Bower always gave time to the visitor. Their larger than life colleague, Bruce Guimaraens, entertained wherever he was. Adrian Bridge, Alistair's son-in-law, continues the tradition.

Reggie Cobb, John Smithies and Felix Vigne, followed by David Orr and Peter Cobb, offered great hospitality, usually without women, at Quinta de Tua.

Alfredo and Jean Hoelzer were often at Quinta de Figuera. Now their son, Johnny, is in charge. Claire Berquvist, full of character, has been followed by her son, Tim Berquist, and in turn by his daughter Sophia, at Quinta de la Rosa.

Fernando van Zeller asked his guests to the elegantly terraced Quinta do Noval, which is now managed by AXA wine supremo Christian Seely.

During vintage time in the sixties, usually during late September and October, the Douro became the fashionable place to be. House party after house party took place with delicious aged tawny port flowing freely. Work was to be done by the few during the day; partying to be done by the many during the night. It was a wonderful sense of achievement when the last grapes were finally gathered and the contents of the last *lagar* trodden. This activity was keenly watched from afar.

The port shippers, back in Blighty, and many a club, livery company, Oxbridge college, city and country wine merchant, were keenly asking, was this going to be a vintage year? The canny port shippers had realised some time ago that they must bide their time before declaring their hands. They had agreed that, by law, the wines must see two winters and a summer before anyone could be confident that the port was of a quality to be considered a vintage port. Also, of course, they could gauge the economic market place by so doing. A vintage port declaration meant money in the pocket for the trade and manifold joy for the consumers, a kind of early win:win.

Writing about my experience in the Douro Valley in 1963, as a naïve, precocious scholar, I stated 'the future of the port trade lies in the stream of samples that are sent to be matched...'. How wonderfully wrong I was. By the mid-1970s, port was mandatorily bottled in Vila Nova de Gaia, brands were becoming king and the old-fashioned merchants' own label ports were dying faster than midges on a steamy August evening on the west coast of Scotland.

In the event, the 1963 vintage was officially declared or registered in the spring of 1965. It was to be one of the greatest years ever. I like to think I contributed in some way, but absolutely nothing comes to mind in the way of evidence...

One wonders sometimes if the port shippers of yore enjoyed their profits more in port glasses than in balance sheets. Percy Croft, whom we have met before, was reported to drink six bottles a day, of his own port. He, rather like Cabel Roope, was 'never quite sober'. Was this carrying quality control a bit far?

In the same era, Wyndham Fletcher, whose great aunt was Ella Cockburn, remembered his original interview with Cockburn's. 'We don't pay much, so I hope you have a private income.' Tim Sandeman told me the story of how he used to commute every day with the same gentleman, in the same carriage, for over twenty years. He was also in the trade and so they talked regularly and became friends. But to Tim's annoyance, the customer never ordered Sandeman's port. Intrigued and not a little frustrated, Tim eventually asked him why not. 'Because you have never asked me to' came the bemused reply. Just as Wyndham Fletcher was apparently told not to mention Cockburn's when he went on the road, so these gentlemen port traders felt awkward closing a deal. They really felt they were purveyors of port, not businessmen in the accepted sense.

Leonard Adams's grandson, David Butler Adams, told me that his grandfather was granted sole supply of wines and spirits to the House of Lords in 1920. To fulfil this prestigious obligation he felt he needed to ship his own vintage port, which Adams did from 1927 to 1966. Not bad years to begin and end on, either.

The only time that I can remember enjoying six bottles of port myself in a day was with five friends. We have met for our annual lunch for nearly forty years. Sadly, we are now five, but at one memorable lunch at Bill Bentleys, Beauchamp Place, we did happily consume, after lunch, six bottles of port. It is all recorded in our JBL book, so it must be true.

Ironically, in those early years, the vintage that I was told to 'purvey' was the illustrious Croft 1963. It was a hard sell, even at £1 per bottle. Today it can be bought for around £85 per bottle ex sales tax and is still delicious. I could say that it was my super salesmanship and their unfettered vision that still enables many of my friends to triumphantly pull a cork or two at special gatherings. In fact, I think it was a very good lunch at the Cavalry Club what did it.

One or two readers may now be nodding or shaking their heads. Nodding if they also bought wisely in yesteryear; shaking at the fact that none of their friends now drink port and they are damned if they are going to open and waste another bottle of their precious vintage port. Those early morning meetings and all those plane trips have led to vintage port becoming an endangered species. Three or four more glasses of red wine would be very nice, thank you, but no port for me, thank you very much. John Mytton would not have been amused.

The real body blow came on 30 June 2007 when the enfeebled government of the day caved in to too many lobby groups. It became illegal for gentlemen, and ladies, to smoke in their own clubs in England. The one time a gentleman really needs a cigar is in his St James's club or city livery hall. How else can you get through the inevitable seven, going on fifteen minutes each, speeches? A glass of vintage port will get him in the mood, whilst a cigar will pull him through. But no more; no more cigars. Speeches seem twice as long. What is more, even when there are no speeches and two or three friends are gathered together and want to relax and unwind, engaging in conversational banter, there is no cigar to measure the length of the conversation. Instead, said friends get up rather awkwardly and melt into the night after a mere glass, rather than the habitual two or three.

As I write, 'elf and safety rules haven't banned port yet. Maybe the decline of our quality of life reflects the decline of port. Common sense and humour are in serious danger of being bureaucrated. The renaissance port person is not having an easy life.

4 THE LONDON BOYS AND THE DOURO BOYS

LET US NOW CONSIDER SOME PORT PEOPLE OF TODAY. All these personalities tend to have a half-full glass rather than a half-empty one. Characters they are; bland they are not.

In the same way that Bordeaux has five first growth Bordeaux estates (Châteaux Lafite Rothschild, Latour, Margaux, Mouton Rothschild and Haut-Brion) and several other great estates knocking on their doors, as it were, it could also be claimed that London has three first growth Royal Warrant-holding wine merchants (Berry Brothers, Corney & Barrow and J&B), with several other great wine merchants knocking on their doors. These would include Lea & Sandeman, Tanners, Goedhuis & Co, Farr Vintners, Wilkinson Vintners, Laytons, Haynes Hanson & Clark and many other such purveyors of excellence.

No one does St James's urbane as well as Hew Blair, Chairman

of Justerini & Brooks, wine merchants to the gentry since 1749. As J&B laconically point out, this was before the United States existed. Justerini's, the company's other shortened name, have always had more than their fair share of characters in their company. It is also said their pale whisky was created so that the womenfolk in the USA could not tell how much was in their husband's glass. Geoffrey Jameson, affectionately nicknamed 'Giant', whose twinkling eyes gave away his wicked sense of humour, Dick Bridgeman, who once drank six double whiskies before a rackets game and won, and Edward Demery, who, like Geoffery, became Clerk to the Royal Cellars, were Hew's predecessors in the boardroom character stakes.

The game of guessing the vintage of the port has been played in J&B's elegant dining room around a round table for over seventy years, firstly in Pall Mall and now in St James's Street in London. 'They (the guests) come for the wine, but remember the port', explains Hew patiently.

For some reason, vintage port has always been singled out for guests to guess. Maybe this stems from the Factory House weekly lunches. There may well be some stunning wines being served, and sometimes guests may be asked their views, but the vintage port is always served 'blind'. I suppose it helps to know that there are a finite number of declared vintages, currently going back to 1875 up to 1997. These are split up between nineteen shippers. So the odds are calculable. But no. This is St James's after all, the

epicentre of nineteenth-century gaming. 'I throw in the odd curly one sometimes, like a single quinta or a late bottle vintage', beams Hew.

Over the years, guests have included cricketers Ted Dexter, David Gower and Allan Lamb, cartoonist JAK, restaurateur Albert Roux, bankers Keswicks and Barings, politicians Jonathan Aitken and Nicholas Soames, plus countless Dukes, Earls, Marquesses and Lords who fortunately only have to sign one name, their surname, after lunch in the series of visitors' books.

The late Queen Elizabeth, The Queen Mother, last lunched there in December 1998. Not for her the nominal £1 bet per person. She upped the ante to £10 per person and promptly guessed the vintage to be the year of her birth, 1900, and happily shovelled her winnings into her lady-in-waiting's handbag. Next stop the bookies?

Almost any excuse to secure a much coveted invitation to J&B is invoked: 'The Friday 13th club', 'The longest day dinner', 'the independent family brewers' are all regulars. All guests participate in the port game. After lunch, upon leaving J&B, there can sometimes be seen mini conspiratorial confessionals on the pavement. With bowed head, one guest will confess that he was in the wrong century, not just the wrong decade, on the port. Hysterical shame is followed by peals of laughter.

The oldest wine merchant to hold a Royal Warrant is Berry Bros. & Rudd, whose amiable chairman is Simon Berry. Number 3 St James's Street, across the road from St James's Palace, has been in the same family for over three hundred years. Before that the site was a real tennis court for Henry VIII. Royal links indeed.

Again it is the visitors' book that provides a focal point. Simon is amazed to discover that his first entry was made when he was two years old! The humble visitors' book links our lives today to the previous generation and earlier. It is truly our link with the past. Lose the visitors' book and you lose a swathe of history. A thank-you email simply does not have, nor will have, the same historical significance as signing your name in such a book.

Unlike Justerini and Brooks, Berrys do not always serve port at lunch. Simon admits that he is 'a great fan of port', but adds that it is almost like a new category. It is not fulfilling its potential in the market-place and it needs energising. We talk about China, as all top wine merchants do these days. Just as Château Lafite Rothschild has become the luxury Bordeaux brand in China, he believes there could be room for one luxury port brand as well. So which is it to be? Which sounds best in Mandarin? Taylor's, Graham's, Fonseca or is there a dark horse coming up on the inside rail?

Back to the visitors' books. We alight on the 1950s one. This was an austerity period as is 2011, but wine merchants like to be optimists. They can enliven both customers and friends with the fruits of their laying down policies. Theirs is a long game. Financing stocks is not for the faint-hearted. Vintage ports are best enjoyed in their adulthood, some even as old age pensioners or senior citizens.

These were typical senior citizens as enjoyed then: Fonseca 1934, Sandeman 1908, Taylor's 1912, 'unknown' 1904, Taylor's 1896, Cockburn 1896, Rebello Valente 1924 and the celebrated Noval 1931. The famous 'Waterloo' Port of 1815 was enjoyed after Château Margaux 1950 and Château d'Yquem 1920. This is history at its best. Nothing speaks to us more clearly than the joys of an old wine. These wines were created more than a century apart. Imagine tasting a wine today that was produced in the Boer War or the Great War. That wine will have innocently witnessed the earliest motor vehicles, men landing on the moon and now Facebook.

Bringing us back to earth, Simon tells me the story of an old and valued customer who always bought vintage port. One day, she was persuaded to buy some late bottled vintage port, which of course had no sediment. Berry's thoughtfully reckoned it would be easier for her to open and enjoy without having to decant each time. In no time at all, she telephoned, sounding stressed and anxious. 'But there is no sediment in this bottle!' she exclaimed. I must have sediment. I like it on my toast.'

Sometimes, you sit uncomfortably in a doctor's waiting room and idly glance at a five-year-old copy of *Hello*. At other times, you could be sitting comfortably in your stockbroker's office recoiling from the latest wealth inducing investment analysis. If, however, you happen to be in City wine merchants Corney & Barrow's elegant reception area, gently succumbing to the joy of a tilting armchair, your hand is subliminally guided to a purple brochure entitled 'The Royal Warrant – a celebration of a time honoured association between Tradesmen and the Monarchy'. The custom of granting royal approval dates back to Henry II's reign in 1155 and numbers expanded hugely under Queen Victoria when over 2,000 warrants were granted. Today there are around 850 Royal Warrant holders and our three first growth wine merchants are amongst this select gathering.

Corney & Barrow's head office in London, is located in an old HM Customs and Excise building built in 1805. Adam Brett-Smith, their debonair managing director, and I are kneeling on the floor, poring over their Vintage Port book. There must be a table somewhere, but we are kneeling happily, tilting our heads from side to side as we study it. The book summarises and analyses in forensic detail each vintage port declaration since 1934. Corney & Barrow are the high priests of vintage port in the UK. The directors, now as then, request samples from all the leading port shippers. They also invite a few 'port noses' to blind taste with their own directors. I became such a port nose for the first time on 5 July 1985, when we tasted the 1983 vintage. It wasn't an earth-moving vintage, more of a gentle kiss vintage. But the sumptuous lunch afterwards made this coveted invitation thoroughly enjoyable.

The previously declared vintage, 1982 (considered to be more like a teenage snog really in the Douro, rather than the adults-only vintage that Bordeaux had enjoyed) had seen the launch of Johnny Graham's new venture, then called Churchill Graham. It did wonderfully well and scored almost top marks. The bottles were then identified. 'Oh no!' exclaimed the firm's then chairman, Keith Stevens. 'We cannot buy this. It is boy's port. Our customers will not wear it. They have not heard of Churchill Graham.' But they did buy. Traditions don't always die hard.

Adam remembers the time when he remonstrated with his chairman about drinking vintage port in the summer instead of a chilled 10-year-old tawny. 'It's a joke. Not in the summer. Far too hot.' said Adam. Keith reflected for a moment. 'If it is a joke, then it is a very good joke.'

Pressed to identify the port drinker of today, Adam indicates that the young Turks of the City are vying with the traditional ducal and gentry customers to be first off the blocks when a new vintage is declared. These rising stars are buying into history and they like the fact that vintage port is not produced every year. This irregularity enhances its reputation. Port is also seen as more virile than Bordeaux. Young Turks need to be virile, otherwise what is the purpose of being one?

Robin Kernick, a past chairman of Corney & Barrow, is an old City Turk and still very much a port person. He remembers the time at Croft's Quinta da Roeda when he was told that one of the workers had been murdered. 'Why, what happened?' he enquired. 'He lacked air' was the laconic rejoinder.

Before I take my leave of Corney & Barrow, another of the directors is asked for his views on port. 'Hangovers', he bellows, 'but I love it.' I think we have all been there. Rather like the hardened sea dog, who is sea sick, but continues to go to sea. It is that stoic, rather masochistic streak in the English character that keeps us enjoying things that sometimes do not enjoy us.

All three of these 'first growth' wine merchants, Justerini & Brooks, Berry Bros. & Rudd and Corney & Barrow have opened up satellite branches in Hong Kong where there is no duty on wine. This of course provides a perfect conduit to China, where real men, and ladies too, may drink port one day.

A healthy tradition of enjoying port has been gently evolving in the USA. My baptism into this world took place in October 1991 when I was asked to join a panel of three at the prestigious biennial *Wine Spectator* New York Wine Experience. For an hour and a half, James Suckling, Marvin Overton and myself smelled, tasted and pontificated to the 1000 guests in front of us. In front of them were 10,000 glasses, a glass for each of the ten ports we were tasting. My memory remains a little hazy except I think we got one or two ports muddled up in our enthusiasm to extol virtue after virtue. But my chief memory is of the end of the session. I knew we had to wrap it up on a high. We were being carried away, as were the other enthusiasts in front of us, by the incredibly georgeous Fonseca 1963. I suddenly spied Bruce Guimaraens sitting modestly ten rows back. Bruce had produced this blockbuster exactly in his own image. I described the wine, looking directly at Bruce, as 'generous, bags of character, balanced fruit, long way to go, made in the image of its winemaker'. Bruce stood up to a richly deserved standing ovation.

The two most prestigious purveyors of wines in New York, to enthusiasts and collectors alike, are Sherry-Lehmann and Morrell. There can be no Royal Warrant holders in the US and it is unlikely that there will ever be President Warrant holders, but if there were, these two would be top contenders. Not far behind are such well-established wine merchants as Zachys and Acker Merrall & Condit on the East Coast and Wally's and K&L on the West Coast. And many more in the states in between.

Sherry-Lehmann, established in 1934, was not named after the sunny town of Jerez, but drew its name from the Louis Sherry building on Madison Avenue. The founding Aaron family were astute enough actually to like wine, post prohibition. After three

locations on Madison, Sherry-Lehmann has recently moved to uber-posh Park Avenue, where their famed original wood panelling has been lovingly installed to endorse their premium position as New York's leading wine merchant. Michael Aaron, now Chairman Emeritus, and his partner Michael Yurch work tirelessly to supply and satisfy New York's insatiable and demanding customers.

Michael Yurch, who is President of Sherry-Lehmann, relates how, in his early days, he once helped a lady who wanted a birthday gift for her husband. The man had been born in a 'difficult' year. 'Young man, 1956 just cannot be an agricultural disaster. It is my husband's birth year and I need to buy him a bottle of port.' If only the Atlantic uncertainty of the Douro's weather pattern could be replaced with the Pacific's regular sunshine in the California region: if only, if only. But where would the fun be in that?

During the prohibition period between 1920 and 1933 in the US, the only wines allowed to be traded were sacramental and medicinal wines, so Morrell's customers tended to be churches, synagogues and physicians. This was an unusual customer base to expand upon, but the company went on to achieve many firsts in the wine trade, amongst which was holding the first fine wine public auction in New York on 29 April 1994.

Morrell, also having moved from Madison Avenue to swanky new offices in the Rockefeller Center, has been led for many years by the visionary Peter Morrell. When asked which was the most memorable wine, not just port, but wine, that he had ever had, he replied with a twinkle in his eye, 'an old tawny from the 1870s or 1880s, shipper unknown'. This from a man who has probably tasted more fine wines than any other top New York wine merchant.

Let us return now to Oporto, where the current heirs and custodians of the early port pioneers are continuously striving to produce wines which all port enthusiasts will like and buy. Still using the first growth analogy, it could be argued that the top three port houses are, alphabetically, Fonseca, Graham's and Taylor's: 'first growths' all three. These and other brands are owned by the two leading port families, the Symingtons and the Robertsons.

Paul Symington is the charming and articulate current senior Sym, joint managing director of the Syms, as everyone affectionately calls them. It is his birthday. Cousins, friends, many of whom are rival port shippers, gather for dinner. Paul is the perfect, hospitable host. Soon we are onto the port, each one tasted blind, naturally. We move seamlessly into Dows 1954 (undeclared), Dow's 1955 through to Quinta da Cavadinha 1978. In normal wine glasses. But we are not asked if we want vintage port. It is part of the dinner and a natural part. It is approachable, inclusive and thoroughly enjoyable. Feeling a little bit like Poirot, I uncover a truth that most have ignored. Serving the ports like this solves the problem of the expected headthrob the following morning. Because they are treated and enjoyed as fine wines, there is, *mon ami*, no headthrob the following morning. Case solved.

Reclining in an armchair in Rupert Symington's office in Vila Nova de Gaia I am reminded of the similarity between the lairds of the Scottish Highlands and the lairds, mostly called Symington, of the Douro highlands. Lairds visit, sometimes stay and have a deep, well-hefted understanding of the land and its people. Lairds also invite guests to share the enjoyment of their estates. Some time ago, two such guests, wine gurus Robert Mondavi and Piero Antinori, swam happily in the Douro whilst enjoying their respective glasses of port.

The Syms are classic Lairds of the Douro. They are the largest vineyard owners with 2,300 acres of vines at twenty-five quintas.

THE SYMINGTONS
THE LAIRDS OF THE DOURO
HIGHLANDS

Think Highlands rather than open flat fields and you will appreciate the grit and determination that has gone into every port bottle, matched by the best British characteristic of a sense of humour. 'A gundog leaped into the *lagar* once whilst treading (the grapes) was in full flow,' laughed Rupert. 'Soon got him out.'

Reclining in another armchair in his cousin Johnny's office, with a log fire blazing away, we were gently interrupted by a delightful PA. Johnny signed a few papers. 'Such is the honour of being the 44th honorary British Consul in Oporto', he smiled. He then added modestly that the first British Consul was his great, great, great, great, great, great, great, great, great, great grandfather Walter Maynard in 1659. They don't heft much greater than that.

These early British Consuls designed whole streets, built hospitals and significantly contributed to society for more than two hundred years. Continuity and strong social values are still vital hallmarks of these active custodians.

Johnny is currently Treasurer of the Factory House. The annual Treasurer's Dinner had just taken place the previous week when the guest of honour was Lord Patten. His parting remark had been, 'As Chancellor of Oxford University, I now know my duty is to continue the great tradition of educating my undergraduates in the benefits of port'. As an aside, we also agreed that for chocoholics like us, the ultimate vinous choice has to be port, with, not instead of, chocolate.

After lunch, another cousin asked Dominic if he was going back to the office. As he had just flown in that morning, he replied in a kind of after lunch port way 'How can I? I haven't been there yet'.

Now we are in Dominic's office, and still reclining. We quickly get onto the subject of Russia, where at a recent port tasting, in a fur coat emporium would you believe, it appears that three drop-dead gorgeous Russian models stripped off, not once, but several times. 'The hazards of the day job,' blinks Dom.

Dom is only too aware that port shippers, like any other business, must always be on the lookout for new markets. It is a question of deformalising the image, whilst maintaining the provenance. Perhaps the Russian format should be adopted in more markets?

The previous Symington generation included Michael, Ian and James. James spent eleven years in the firm's tasting room.

Imagine. A nightmare or the ultimate dream? He recollects his father shooting snipe in his waders, in wet fields at the bottom of their garden near Oporto before breakfast. Also, there were weekend partridge shoots and the occasional wild boar shoot in the Douro. James echoes what many who are born into the port trade think. He sums it up: 'It is genuinely not so much a business as a way of life.'

The Douro acts as a magnet. The darkness and the silence at night turn into sunshine and gaiety during the day, in much the same way as they do in the Highlands and Islands of Western Scotland. Having stayed at their family quinta in the Douro for the second time, Sir John Major endorsed this sentiment by confiding in James that his two favourite places to stay the weekend 'were Balmoral and Malvedos'.

In Vila Nova de Gaia, a typical cobbled winding road connects parts of the two leading port houses, the Symingtons and the Taylor Fladgate partnership. It is called Rua Rei Ramiro and halfway between the two is a nightclub, the Rocks Fashion Dance Club. I have absolutely no idea what goes on behind these shuttered doors, but I do know what goes on behind those of the port lodges on either side. Hundreds, probably thousands, of casks or pipes of port are slumbering silently, enjoying a kind of very, very extended afternoon nap. What is wonderful to the passer-by, is that each cask exudes its own delicious aroma so that a pungent mix of stimulating, sensual fragrances wafts back and forth up and down the street. I was immediately struck by the similarity to those coffee advertisements on the television. What a wonderful way to advertise the delights of port.

Adrian Bridge, managing director of the Fladgate Partnership, greets me in the foyer of The Yeatman, his stunning new luxury hotel set high above the Douro in Vila Nova de Gaia. Adrian is the Robertson's son-in-law. Focused and determined, he has diversified in a major way by designing and building this world-class hotel. Yet his guidelines for The Yeatman invoke the same sense of fair play and generosity that runs through the port shipper's mindset. For example, his hotel stocks all his competitors' ports. He also offers a stupendous range of Portuguese table wines, even though his company has no

financial interest in any of them. This generosity allows him to become a champion for all Portugal in a thoroughly eclectic way. Authenticity, individuality and care for the environment were the guiding principles in the creation of this hotel complex.

Adrian thrives on challenges. Not content with merely creating a new port category, pink port, he has yomped bottles of his Croft Pink up mountains and carved out an armchair in ice in Antarctica so that he could relax with a pink port in the snow. Pink, or rosé, port could well become as popular as rosé or pink champagne. Most champagne houses initially scoffed at Laurent Perrier's 'rosé'. Now they are all at it. Fashion has become style. Pink port may succeed where white port has not. I cannot wait for a 10-year-old pink port. That would get the armchair wallahs gasping, unless of course they were already in Antarctica.

Adrian tells me a racy story about his erstwhile partner, the late Bruce Guimaraens: 'He always maintained that the best way to judge the quality of the new vintage was to lick the fresh must off a nubile young girl's bare leg in the lagar.'

Alistair Robertson, Adrian's father-in-law, is really more at home in a comfortable armchair with a glass of red port. Not outdone by his son-in-law, Alistair himself had also created a new easy-to-drink style, a filtered, non-sediment Late Bottled Vintage, in 1970. This was in response to The Savoy's gentle moan that their customers would like a less expensive port, which didn't need ageing or financing so much, but which still tasted like vintage port. Taylor's LBV was thus filtered, fined and bottled, ready to drink. But like the pink port concept years later, some jeers came before the plaudits in trad Gaia.

Alistair had originally been called to Oporto as a business doctor. He was enjoying a leisured lifestyle in Scotland when a cousin unexpectedly handed him the keys to one of the port trade's best loved names, Taylor's. This was in the 1960s when it was still touch and go as to whether the port trade would ever make a comeback after the parlous state of all economies and specifically, in port's case, after the traditional 'upstairs downstairs' lifestyle had disappered.

Together with his two partners, Huyshe Bower and Bruce Guimaraens, Alistair gradually turned the business round. This quietly outspoken port ambassador is, like Paul Symington, equally clear that 'port is a wine extension'. 'Port must be brought more into the meal', they both chorus.

Johnny Graham is the port trade's self-effacing true entrepreneur. He is also probably regarded as the trade's most experienced taster. Not able to use his own surname for business reasons, he happily trades under his wife's maiden name, Churchill.

Johnny, like all his friends and rivals, is thoughtful about the future of port. How best can they stimulate their target market? We talk about the phenomenal success of the television series *Downton Abbey*. 'Why don't you ask Julian Fellowes to include the guessing-the-vintage-port game in his next series?' we suggest. Product placement. As Oscar Wilde memorably remarked 'There is only one thing worse than being talked about and that is not being talked about'.

If Johnny Graham is the entrepreneur, Robin Reid, from the slightly older generation, is the raconteur. Robin has spent his life with Croft and his stories are legend. There is, for example, the local Douro farmer, whose day job was as a taxi driver, who sold several pipes or barrels of 60-year-old port to Robin after much haggling. He kept several back. Robin used to invite the farmer downriver to Vila Nova de Gaia to taste his ports, to see how they were getting on. After a time, the distraught farmer unburdened himself to Robin. 'Senhor Reid. Their brothers are missing their siblings. I must immediately sell you the remaining pipes – at no extra cost. Then they will all be together…'!

Writers and story tellers loved staying in the Douro. Somerset Maugham, Dennis Wheatley, E. M. Forster and Hilaire Belloc – 'a funny little man with a celluloid collar' – all appreciated the desolate, but hospitable quintas. The Douro seems to bring out the happy schoolboy in almost anyone.

Robin, incidentally, was also a first-class shot in his day. He well remembers walking-up days with bags of thirty to forty red-leg partridges in the Douro and sixty to seventy snipe days shooting from his boat in the Aveiro marshes, south of Oporto. After a recent lunch with Robin, he poured each of us a glass of 10-year-old tawny. Leaning back in his armchair, sighing contentedly, he smiled. 'Port fills the soul. At least it fills mine.'

Peter Cobb, a former director of Cockburn's, is astonished at the turnaround in the fortunes of port and sherry. During his forty years in the port and sherry trade, sherry has declined from twenty million cases to five million cases a year. Port has increased from three million cases to ten million cases, in round figures.

A major turning point for port came when Guy Ritchie's father John, Madonna's ex father-in-law, and a partner in Cockburn's advertising agency, launched Cockburn's Special Reserve in a television advertising campaign at Christmas 1969. Success was immediate and Cockburn's became brand leader overnight. But volume was king and when Cockburn's failed to declare the great 1977 vintage, their quality star waned. 'Twenty years on, ramifications will be felt,' predicted Peter at the time, and how right he was.

A father and daughter team, Tim and Sophia Bergqvist's family have owned their delightful Quinta de la Rosa for over one hundred years. Perhaps not quite in the league of the early port pioneers, but a hundred years, continuous ownership of anything is not to be sneezed at. Tim's mother, the formidable Claire, always served borscht soup when she entertained at her generous dinner parties. Sometimes the beetroot borscht was not to everyone's liking and it simply got flung out of the open windows on to the garden below. Imagine our horror when we passed the next day after one such summer dinner. 'What is this battlefield?' exclaimed someone, who had not been at the previous night's dinner, seeing all the plants and flowers seemingly covered with blood.

Perhaps appropriately, next enter the Douro Boys. Not the stars of a Western film shot in rugged Portugal, not the magnificent seven, but rather the five musketeers. These five Portuguese characters, a multi-talented winemaking phenomenon, have seen the future and it is not only port that the Douro must continue to produce, but red, rosé and white wine. Bashful they are not. They became known as the 'The Douro Boys' after a Swiss wine journalist met them all and wrote about these 'boys from the Douro'. The English name stuck even though they thought they might be confused with a boy band.

Cristiano van Zeller, one of the original members of this merry group, tells me that emails between the five got even more hilarious when they learnt that a Spanish wine journalist could not understand why she had to interview these five Douro Boys as, apparently, 'boys' in vernacular Spanish means male strippers. Douro Boys they are; Chippendales they ain't. It is difficult to imagine 'The Loire Boys' or 'The Bordeaux Boys' but maybe sherry could follow? 'The Oloroso Boys' or 'The Manzanilla Girls' perhaps?

These five friends, owning five great wine estates between them, decided to band together to promote their products. Since 2003, they have travelled the world, five Portuguese chaps having fun, selling some wine and making friends in the tradition of the original Douro pioneers. Cristiano also mentioned that ladies are an integral part of this mix. Not only does he employ three women oenologists, but what is the point of making great wine unless everyone can enjoy it together?

The sea change of 'direct sales' only became possible in 1986, when the law allowed individual estates or quintas to export direct instead of going through the bureaucratically controlled customs zone in Vila Nova de Gaia. Since the 1990s these five leading estates have specialised in Douro wine. Of course all involved love their port, but great ports tend to have English or British sounding names. These are top *terroir* ports and wines, produced in small quantities by those in the know. There are 33,000 wine growers in the Douro and eighty per cent own less than half a hectare each.

The Douro Boys' estates are:

1. **Quinta do Vallado**, established in 1716, which is managed by Joao Ferreira Alvares Ribeiro, he with a special sense of humour, and his cousin Francesco Ferreira; 70 hectares.

2. **Quintas de Napoles and do Caril**, dating back to 1496, owned by Dirk Niepoort, 'who ought to be designated a world heritage site himself'. Dirk's first red wine was in 1990; 25 hectares.

3. **Quinta do Crasto**, founded in 1615, is owned by the Roquette family, Jorge with his twinkling generosity and son Miguel with musketeer good looks. First red wine produced in 1994; 70 hectares.

4. **Quinta do Vale Dona Maria** is run by the charismatic and larger than life Cristiano van Zeller. His wife Joana's family have owned the quinta for over two hundred years. First red wine in 1996; 21 hectares.

5. **Quinta do Vale Meao**, registered since 1877, is now managed by Francisco Javier de Olazabal, who is the great-grandson of the formidable Dona Antonia Adelaide Ferreira, the quinta's original owner. First red wine in 1999; 67 hectares.

5 ANY TIME, ANYWHERE... ANYBODY

AT THE END OF A GOOD DINNER WITH CLOSE FRIENDS, there is something wonderfully civilised, albeit a little bit naughty, about the sight of a full decanter of port on your host's sideboard. The anticipation of the shuffling of chairs and the closing in, conspiratorially, on your host, is very enticing, as the ladies withdraw.

Just before this ritual, the gallant gentlemen will have shown their love, admiration and respect for the fairer sex by standing up. Recognising the ladies' insatiable need to powder and gossip, they will have bid them a lingering *au revoir*. It is this gentlemanly gesture that so strongly endears the gentler, fairer sex to us. After all, our ever-lovings would not wish their men folk to simply sit and do nothing in their absence, now would they? Men should be allowed their port moments, as women are allowed their blonde ones...

So, wearyingly understanding, denying themselves the hot coffee and luxury chocolates next door, the gentlemen pass the port, round and round and round. Far racier stories are often told by the womenfolk next door, whilst the men consider the horrors of the recession. On many occasions, we all like sitting together to enjoy the port, but some of us like to be a bit old-fashioned once in a while, to the obvious relief of our long suffering 'wags'. As Auberon Waugh once pointed out, 'Women still regard port as their natural enemy'.

Whether consumed separately or together, proper port works wonders for the soul. If the wine during dinner has been mature old world, then it is thoroughly beneficial for both sexes' digestions to follow through with a proper glass or two of mature port. If, on the other hand, the wine during dinner has been some over-alcoholised new world confection, then everyone needs a proper glass or two of mature port to get their gastric juices back into equilibrium.

Port has a unique, affectionate place in many men's private cellar of thoughts. This joyful liquid thread that joins together like-minded men, and plenty of ladies too, somehow enables conversation to be on a higher plane than if the same people were ordering pints of lager standing at a bar. When you drink port, you tend to be sitting down (or in extreme cases, lying down). By passing the port you are offering your next door neighbour a drink. This is even more wonderful when you are not paying for it. Your tummy is replete, overlayered with vinous pleasures. No wonder the conversation flows as fast or, in some houses, faster than the decanter.

At this point George Meredith's now neglected comic novel *The Egoist* has the perfect duologue between guest and host, illustrating so well the juxtapositioning of pressure, reluctance and gracious, grateful and well-timed surrender of two port people.

'Another bottle is to follow.'
'No!'
'It is ordered.'
'I protest.'

'It is uncorked.'
'I entreat.'
'It is decanted.'
'I submit...'

The same chapter contains the happiest definition of a wine cellar. 'Cellars are not catacombs. They are, if rightly constructed, rightly considered cloisters where the bottle meditates on joys to bestow, not on dust misused.'

I also feel, rather strangely maybe, that Peter York struck a 'port persona' chord with his readers, when he co-wrote the original Sloane Ranger handbook. York recently revisited his Sloane world. He wrote ' Sloanes mostly descended from 19th century, moderate, Forsyte-ish success, public school expansion, the Empire, the Armed forces, C of E, Oxbridge, the Law and Parliament's back benches.

'But in the 21st century, which looks to Bill Gates and Lakshmi Mittal as role models... The rising popularity of vaguely, safely Sloane preppy brands such as Boden and OKA suggest people find the old symbols reassuring in tough times'.

Kind of sums it up, really.

But what of those people who decline the offer of port? These same people will often readily accept a further three or four glasses of your red wine. What can the host, who has a cellar full of Croft 1963 or Fonseca 1977 for example, do? I have the answer.

Many years ago, the owner of the renowned Scott's Restaurant of Mayfair wanted to stage a promotion. The idea was that I would open a bottle or two of vintage port with port tongs and Ross Benson, the noted diary columnist, would then write about this rather extreme sport. I had never touched port tongs, let alone used them, but they are very useful if you have forgotten your corkscrew. I duly had a lesson at Alistair Robertson's (owner of Taylor's) house in Vila Nova de Gaia. He had never used them either. We looked at each other, then bravely plunged the tongs into the roaring log fire until the ends got red-hot. I clamped them to the neck of the chosen bottle. Amazingly, the neck, with the cork still inside, sheared off completely cleanly and we were able to decant the vintage port quite normally.

Thus rehearsed, back at Scotts, I tonged two bottles of vintage port at about 6pm one weekday. The restaurant was not full, hence the need for the promotion. Ross, Nicky the owner and I exchanged glances. What now? We decided to attack the two bottles of Taylor's 1970 and 1975 that I had just decanted. Two hours later, the two bottles were nearly empty and we had never felt so good. As Ross succinctly put it, 'I have never before drunk and enjoyed port when I have been sober'.

So that was a bit of a revelation. The French, of course, do drink port as an aperitif, in the same way that we used to drink sherry. (One Frenchman who was a celebrated port lover was Toulouse-Lautrec. The only trouble was that his favourite way of drinking it was mixed with garlic, as a cure for chronic bronchitis. According to the poet Paul Leclercq, he always had on him 'a small grater and nutmeg with which he scented the ports he drank... He tasted old vintages as a connoisseur.') To encourage the non-port drinkers, perhaps the answer is to give your guests an unexpected pleasure early in the evening. When you have decanted the port, and just as they are looking forward to their first libation from your cellar, proffer them a taste of vintage port.

I think proffering rather than offering, as this means they can't really refuse. They will be overcome with your generosity and feel rather smug, as though they have done something really rather naughty. Your guests will then much look forward to enjoying this *vinho generoso* when the time comes. A teaser for the main feature, perhaps?

Port is probably the first wine brand that we islanders ever knew. Claret and sherry, yes, but they were definitely 'foreign'. Port became our wine, rather as cricket became our sport all those years ago. There is something very English, that can't be replicated, that ties port to cricket. Surely WG must have enjoyed port? Hutton, Cowdrey, Compton, Dexter read just as well as Taylor's, Graham's, Croft and Warre's.

Sir John Major, who famously described the country that we all know and love in full Betjeman mode, 'Fifty years from now Britain will still be the country of long shadows on cricket grounds, warm beer...', confided to me that he enjoyed his port. I am sure that he would really have preferred a glass of chilled tawny port to a pint of warm beer. John Major, with his firm handshake, looks you straight in the eye. He is a gentlemanly port person.

Fittingly, there is an excellent cricket pitch at the Oporto Cricket and Lawn Tennis Club. In September 1989, Tim Stanley Clarke, the port trade's favourite PR, organised a cricket match between the then English Test captain, David Gower, and his touring party XI versus the Oporto Cricket and Lawn Tennis Club's XI. The former included fellow Test cricketer Allan Lamb and actor Dennis Waterman. The latter included any member of the port trade who could pick up a bat and run with it.

A limited bottling of Dow's 20-year-old tawny, 'The Captain's

Port', was presented to us players, complete with signatures on the back label. The following day we boarded a train from Oporto to Pinhao in the middle of the desolate but beautiful Douro Valley. As the trail trundled alongside the River Douro, the guard's van seamlessly became our moving cricket pitch. Three Bollinger bottles, empty by then, became the stumps. Bats appeared. Random tennis balls became cricket balls. These were then mercilessly struck out of the stifling guard's van into the unsuspecting countryside and even into the river itself. Totally unprepared were the Portuguese passengers sitting three carriages back, who were interrupted every minute or so by tousle-haired Englishmen charging through the train, ready to unleash the ball as they entered the guard's van. I received a black eye as I misjudged a ball bowled Gower, batted Lamb. I don't think my wife believes me to this day.

Let us consider another of life's great conundrums. Why is it that we can consume vast quantities of wine when we are in a particular wine region with absolutely no ill-effect and yet, back home during the week, we simply cannot? The argument that certain wines don't travel is, of course, complete bunkum. It is we who find our gastric juices change with different expectations and environments.

I put this soul-searching question to Hugh Johnson, the world's leading wine writer. He thought for a second, then looking me straight in the eye, said 'I think we need a serious sponsor to enable us to spend long enough in these wine regions to thoroughly research this question, don't you?'

During a Brooks's annual wine visit to Oporto in May 2008, one fellow member turned to me and admitted, to his great astonishment, that of all his visits to many different wine regions all over the world, on a day-to-day basis he had enjoyed the clearest head on this port trip. I can readily affirm that many glasses were proffered and few refused during the four days.

On the same basis, good wine really does taste better when it has been brought up directly from the wine producer's cellar. Apart from lying undisturbed at the right temperature, it is somehow harmoniously hefted to the terroir. I hope there is not a scientific explanation for this. It would be nice just to believe it through experience.

There seems to be a mysterious ratio between being relaxed in the fresh air, in a foreign country, enjoying glass after glass after glass and being in work mode at home, in a city and just enjoying a glass or two, maximum. Of course the weekend is the halfway house. There is that magical moment on a Friday evening, well away from the dreaded emails, when one gently opens the cellar door. Descending the stairs, quivering with anticipation, one ambles over to the port bins. Which one tonight, Josephine? Once chosen, the lucky bottle is carefully brought upstairs to stand upright, so he can shake himself down a bit, ready to be given some fresh air when opened the following day. Saturday evenings, after a bit of sport, real or on television, are the perfect times to enjoy real men's pleasure. Sunday mornings are, after all, Sunday mornings.

Any port in a storm: what a sensible notion. Once I found myself sitting, as one does, cross-legged on the tarmac outside Athens airport in over 100° heat. My new best friend turned out to be a famous Greek wine importer. Well, we were both thirsty. One of us would have had to get up and buy some overpriced water.

Instead I opened my suitcase and took out a bottle of rather warm Croft 10-year-old tawny, with a stopper cork, so sensible. A 10-year tawny port, one of life's great enhancers, is always best served chilled. But, as I said, any port in a storm. We glugged it down joyfully and launched the product in Greece a few months later. (I think this is why I so enjoyed the film *Sideways*.)

Those 10-year aged tawny ports are versatile creatures. It is no coincidence that St James Church in Oporto, which serves the British community, uses them as its communion wine. I have helped a friend carry a six pack through its hallowed doors. Recently, a wine trade friend told me that he supplies ruby port to his church in Yorkshire. Colder there, the congregation need more robust central heating.

To embrace this religious link, I remember attending a senior, but raucous dinner on a Saturday night at Trinity College, Cambridge, in the 1960s. For some reason there was some 1924 vintage port left over. Perhaps it wasn't that raucous an evening. The 1924 port was duly served, to a full house, at communion the following morning. I think a few of us were more focused on *Oliver Twist* than we should have been.

I may have made up the saying, 'All great wine would like to be bottled in magnums if it could'. What potentially pretty girl would not wish to show herself off in the best possible light? Great wine or port takes a little bit longer to mature (get herself ready, as it were) and improve (with experience) and we, the consumers (lovers) are the beneficiaries.

I am sometimes asked that most vexing of questions, 'What is the oldest wine you have ever drunk?' Vexing because the oldest is not necessarily the best, and age itself is rather irrelevant.

In some underground cellars that I have been privileged to visit, I have been offered very old wine of which not even the offeror could know the date.

My mind rushes back to splendid old butts of manzanilla in Sanlúcar de Barremeda or of fino in Jerez de la Frontera. Both are solera wines that may contain some sherries a century old, or even more. Another that really stands out in my memory is a magical bottle of Tokayi Essencia 1904, which I shared with Lord Rothschild when he opened it for his cousin Baroness Philippine de Rothschild at Waddesdon. I have just been to my dining room and had another sniff at the open bottle of Boal 1841 that I keep on the sideboard for such emergencies.

In answer to the 'oldest bottle' question I usually settle for a bottle of port that I bought at Sothebys for £4. It was a Morgan 1881. I was intrigued because Morgan Brothers, long established since 1715, had been bought by Croft, so it was kind of in the family. It was also rare, very old and quite cheap. I opened the bottle exactly a hundred years after its conception, on Christmas day 1981. My family were also intrigued because it was certainly the oldest bottle they had ever seen. The wonderful thing was that you had to be quite quick about it. Five minutes to allow the bottle stink to disappear – the equivalent of b.o., having been trapped in a container for a very long time; twenty minutes of sheer vinous pleasure; and then sudden death. The living wine dusted itself down, dressed for the occasion and then, like one's favourite granny, elegantly, but firmly went upstairs.

At this age, port is wine. It leaves its fortified nature behind. We were, in effect, drinking an occasion, a window of history. Its elegant charm and velvet complexity totally shut out the mundane nature of everyday life. It was a transcendental moment, whatever that is, and then back to the washing up.

Port's longevity enables the consumer, you and me, to combine history and the present, as few other wines, or for that matter, foods, can. As George Meredith puts it, again in *The Egoist*: 'Port is deep – sea deep. We cannot say that of any other wine. Port is our noblest legacy. I cherish the fancy that port speaks the sentences of wisdom. It is in its flavour deep; mark the difference. It is like a classic tragedy, organic in conception... retaining the strength of youth with the wisdom of age...'

Queen Victoria and Prime Minister William Gladstone were in charge of our island and empire when these grapes were picked and trodden in that remote and desolate valley in northern Portugal. We had enjoyed the same grapes, admittedly with added value, exactly one hundred years later, when Queen Elizabeth II and Prime Minister Margaret Thatcher were in charge of our island, but no longer an empire.

This simple bottle of port, with its deep red grapes grown on steep terraces and picked by hand, with its original hand-blown bottle and long cork hewn from the oak forests of the Alentejo in southern Portugal, had been lying down on its side, silently sleeping, whilst the world fought wars, invented motor cars and went to the moon. It woke up and enjoyed, I hope, its twenty minutes of fame. Uniquely, it linked the generations in the same way that grandparents can do so successfully.

There is a story of a well-known shot who once accepted a friend's invitation to a 200-bird day. Another friend rang to ask him for a 300-bird day, on the same day. The shot accepted the latter. Another friend rang minutes later to ask him for a 400-bird day, on the same day. The shot accepted the latest, better invitation. The day before the shoot, the last friend called to say that the day had been cancelled. The whole thing had been a massive leg-pull that caused much merriment in the shires.

But my point is, would it not be marvellous if a friend rang up asking you for dinner and dangled a 1977 vintage port in front of you? Then another friend telephoned asking you for the dinner the same day, but slid in to the conversation that the 1963 was being prepared. And then, and then, a third friend called to ask you on the exact same day and breathed down the receiver that the 1945 was going to be decanted especially for you. Cripes. This would be blood pressure stuff, glorious wishful thinking. Of course manners maketh man, especially a port person, so how bad could your 'cold' be, how necessary is it that you attend that 'aged aunt's funeral'?

My personal contribution to the Thatcher years was vital, but not widely appreciated. My very good friend Lord Denham and his very good friend Lord Soames were respectively Chief Whip and Leader of the House of Lords. These were testing times and testing times need lubrication. I regularly used to pop a couple of cases of 20-year-old tawny port into the boot of my car. Occasionally, if times were really testing, their Lordships used to upgrade to 30-year-old tawny ports. I would drive into their Lordships' car park, carry the cases past happy saluting doormen, up the stairs and into their offices. As Christopher Soames and Bertie Denham so successfully proved over many years, you do not have to wait for a special occasion to enjoy these wondrous riches. Their subtle pleasures help conversation and may even win you the argument. So, when you yourself feel that you want to open a bottle, just open it.

Whisky and cognac producers let it be known, usually to explain their pricing structure, that they lose up to three per cent per annum of their spirit when it is maturing in cask, due to evaporation. Rather romantically, they call this 'the angels' share'.

Port can also evaporate. But this is called 'the butler's share' and it is otherwise known as nicking, in the nicest possible way. I have witnessed this first-hand in a traditional Hampshire cellar. The port, a rare Rebello Valente 1931, was double binned, i.e. rows were stacked one behind the other. Hundreds upon hundreds of bottles were neatly cellared thus. The front bins were all present and correct. The back bins were, to a bin, empty. Over forty years, the butler had drunk the lot. In another cellar, in another county, the butler had carefully and systematically removed the two bottles of vintage port that were concealed behind the slate pad that indicated the name and vintage of the port in that particular bin. Both master and butler agreed that in future it would be better for both parties if the former took back possession of the cellar door key...

The subject of butlers somehow leads on to toastmasters. The vast majority of loyal toasts used to be made in port, some still are, whilst others seem to be made when the glass is empty. Port, however, is the traditional British way to toast the Royal Family. Most banqueting port glasses are too small. This is a serious problem for the serious port drinker. Those ridiculous elgin sherry glasses (the waisted ones) surely accelerated sherry's downfall. Proper port needs to be swirled, swilled and seduced in a proper glass.

What is the best port glass? A clear glass that is clean, and large enough to enable the aromas to develop and the port itself to breathe. To present itself in the best possible way to the consumer. A glass that is too small does the port no justice at all. Better a white wine glass every time than a mean apology for a port glass. Elgin glasses should be smashed on sight!

George Riedel, the revolutionary Austrian wine glass producer, set about producing the optimum port glass in the 1980s. I was invited to attend the 'tasting'. The same wines really did taste different in different glasses. Not only that, but the development of vintage port in the glass was much more pronounced than 10- and 20-year aged tawny ports. The reason is logical. Mature vintage port has often been stuck in a glass container, a bottle, for twenty, thirty years or more. Finally released, boy does it stretch its arms, its legs, you name it, it stretches it. All this stretching makes it a very different wine after a few minutes. By contrast, the 10- and 20-year aged tawny ports have been gently slumbering in their own wooden containers, casks, for the same number of years, enabling them to mature more quickly during this same period. Hence their name, aged tawny, due to their loss of colour through the oak. When these wines hit the glass, there is much less evolution in the wine.

Fearlessly, I championed the unthinkable at the tasting. Riedel must create two port glasses. One for vintage port, with a more open bowl to let the wine breathe more fully, the other for aged tawny port, with a more restrained opening to conserve the already more developed aroma and bouquet.

Glasses must be clean, as I said. By that I mean clean of outside smells, not of course clean as in dry clean. A very old friend entertained the great and the good generously and often. Invariably, at The Old Rectory, he would serve them the Croft 1963 that he had bought from me after a very good luncheon at the Cavalry Club. He telephoned me one day in high dudgeon. And Angus in high dudgeon was quite high enough for me. 'Your' (note that it was mine, not his) 'port has gone off. I serve it to my friends and they reject it.' One thing of which I am absolutely certain is that Croft 1963 is never 'off'. Bottled long before cork tainted bottles had made their appearance, you will often get bottle variations, but never a port that is 'off'. Bottle variations occur because we all age differently and port sure is a living thing, so it does too.

I accepted Angus's subsequent kind invitation to dinner. We had lots of lovely wine and then the port decanter hove into view. I must admit that I wasn't paying huge attention to this part of the proceedings, as the lady on my left was beautiful and intriguing. I had rather forgotten about my host's dudgeon. I wafted my port glass upwards to my rarefied nose. 'God' I think I grimaced, but it could have been much, much worse. My host had been watching from his end of the dining-room table. 'There you are', he triumphantly cried, 'told you!' One thing I was equally clear about was that this was not Croft 1963. We eventually traced the culprit – the innocent port glass. Poor thing. Together with its siblings it had been continually washed in the dishwasher with some powder that seriously affected it and stuck to the inside of the glass. Then the glasses were placed upside down on the shelves of an enclosed wooden cupboard. This was the last straw for them. The clinging aroma of detergent was trapped. Thus clean had become dirty.

A few random musings to end this chapter. The Navy has a toast for each day. Friday is 'Foxhunting and old port'. Saturday is 'Sweethearts and wives and may they never meet'. Clearly this is a variation on a girl in every port and a port in every girl.

To lower the tone further, a gentleman, slightly the worse for wear, lurched into the fashionable Admiral Codrington pub in Chelsea. Trying to concentrate by closing one eye and then the other, he surveyed the different drinks behind the bar. Taking his time, he eventually decided on port and asked the barman what port did he have? 'The nearest port is Southampton, and the next ferry is at three pm, now eff off', rejoined the exasperated barman.

'An old Gourmet who's grown somewhat stout,
Felt a twinge and much feared it was gout,
'If I drink now,' he thought,
Three whole bottles of port,
It will surely settle the doubt.'

So spake the great Yorick.

As long ago as 1584, Thomas Cogan had claimed 'Drink wine, and have the gout; drink none, and have the gout'. Gout, from the Old French *goute* meaning drop, is a metabolic disorder, the first sign of which is often extreme pain in the innermost joint of the big toe. Men over forty are usually in the firing line and it was always assumed that it was over-indulgence that caused it. Hence gout became known as a disease of the aristocracy or the 'rich man's disease'. In 1885, the *New York Times* ran a headline 'Port wine a cure for gout, a medicine by no means unpleasant.' Havelock Ellis wrote in *A study of British Genius* in 1904 that gout was an indication of 'preeminent intellectual ability'. In *The Devil's Dictionary* in 1906, Ambrose Bierce defined gout as 'a physician's name for the rheumatism of a rich patient'. However recent research has shown that gout is not caused by port, but by excess uric acid, more prevalent in beer and spirits. Hoorah for research. Indeed, teetotallers and vegetarians also suffer from the disease. Very recent research suggests that cherries might help guard against gout. Double hoorahs.

Charles Dickens in *The Pickwick Papers* beautifully highlights the dilemma of the other frequent misconception.

'Is anything the matter with Mr Snodgrass, sir?' enquired Emily, with great anxiety.

'Nothing the matter, ma'am,' replied the stranger. 'Cricket dinner – glorious party – capital songs – old port – claret – very good – wine, ma'am – wine.'

'It wasn't the wine,' murmured Mr Snodgrass, in a broken voice. 'It was the salmon.'

Somehow or other, it never is the wine, in these cases.

I was dining once with Steven and Bella Spurrier at their apartment in Paris. Steven, one of the wine trade's undoubted gentlemen and ever the wine enthusiast, had opened a few magnums of fabulous *cru classe* Bordeaux, as was his generous wont. Suddenly he leapt to his feet. 'I know,' he cried, 'we need some old tawny port now.' None was in the cellar. Undeterred, he mounted his bicycle and set off into the twilight. Fortunately, his wine shop was not too far away. He swooped a bottle of Croft 30-year-old tawny port off his shelf, nestled it in his carrier basket and rode triumphantly home. Minutes later, the three of us were happily contemplating a half-full bottle. Or was it a full empty bottle? Steven had made the occasion special.

6
ONE
OVER
THE TEN

Lists seem to have evolved from the humble shopping list to the 'celebrity' must have, must do, lists. Ever one to avoid a trend, I offer you below my own lists about port, which could easily be regarded as shopping lists anyway.

We have already ascertained that Port's natural number is eleven. So here are eleven port types.

1. BLUE CHIP PORTS.

The best and most sought-after names. The classic investment buy, but at least drink some.

FONSECA

Fonseca is not the most English of names, but, by golly, it offers arguably the most English of characteristics. The ultimate port person's port, Fonseca vintage ports have an inner core which never diminishes. The sheer luxury of the full flavours bewitches, enhances and satisfies the fortunate consumer in spades. Quinta do Panascal is the key vineyard here.

The investment markets like the brand. It is always top end.

The Guimaraens family firm started life as Fonseca, Monteiro & Co. They always used the Fonseca name for their vintage port labels. I suppose the anglicised Guimaraenses reckoned that the diehard English colonel in his club would find it easier to pronounce Fonseca than their own family name. I certainly do.

Since 1896, well over a hundred years, only four members of the Guimaraens family have been continuously responsible for their vintage ports, which must be a record. Frank from 1896–1948, his daughter Dorothy in 1955, Bruce, great-grandson of the founder, from 1960–1992 and his son, David, from 1994 to the present day. (The in-between years were not 'declared vintage' years for Fonseca.) Continuity of excellence and style over the generations has simply paid off.

Bruce Guimaraens, sadly no longer with us, was the epitome of the perceived view of the British port shipper. Both *vinho* and *generoso* could well have been tailor- (or Taylor-) made for this larger than life character. He inspired friendship, respect and loyalty. He led legions of visitors to a particular bar, the Perla Negra in Oporto, just to check out the distribution of his ports.

The Guimaraens family sold their firm to Taylor's in 1948, thus uniting two highly sought-after, yet very different, port houses and brands. Extrovert joined elegance to make excellence.

BRUCE
GUIMARAENS

GRAHAM

Graham: a straightforward enough name. When juxtaposed next to the words vintage port, however, Graham takes on a reverence and blue chip investment status at the highest level, especially when you add the tantalising initials 'W & J' before it.

Originally Scottish, this firm consistently produces wonderfully complex powerful vintage ports that last decades and never seem to lose their fruit. James Suckling of *Wine Spectator* magazine describes Graham vintage ports as having a 'high concentration of ripe fruit and an iron backbone of tannins'. Quinta dos Malvedos is the dominant vineyard.

W&J Graham was established in Oporto as a textile woollen company in 1806. They started shipping port in 1820 because they had accepted a few pipes of port in settlement of an outstanding debt. Fortunately for us, from this accidental start, the firm decided to stay in the port trade. The Graham family sold out to the embracing Symingtons one hundred and fifty years later. The Syms have nurtured this brand well and it is always in the frame.

The Symington port producers of today are the twelfth and thirteenth generations since their direct ancestors, Walter Maynard, Henry Wittingham and Samuel Palmer, helped start the great tradition of port production.

Even today, one of Oporto's smartest suburbs, where one of the Graham establishments was located, is known as 'O Graham'. The works football team at another of Graham's Oporto factories was to become Portugal's first football club, Boavista.

TAYLOR'S

Top wineries often seem to reflect their owners. Baron Eric de Rothschild is unmistakably Lafite – both being very elegant. Baroness Philippine de Rothschild is unmistakably Mouton – both being very extrovert. Alistair Robertson has made Taylor's his own – both very elegant. Whereas his late partner, Bruce Guimaraens, had made Fonseca his own – both being big and extrovert.

Taylor's, or Taylor Fladgate & Yeatman to give it its full title, surged into first growth status generations ago. They have consistently produced great raw material from their beloved vineyard, Quinta da Vargellas, and then they have had very focused marketing.

When young, Taylor's vintage ports have a dry hardness to their backbone. This translates into balanced fruity elegance on maturity. There is something slightly superior about Taylor's vintage ports. Others often seek this, but seldom achieve it.

The firm was founded in 1692 by one of the earliest port traders, Job Bearsley. His 4XX mark, originally a woolmark, is still cut into the walls of the Casa dos Alambiques where Taylor's have made wine from 1744 to this day (apart from a short break as a field hospital for Wellington's troops). The triple name was created in 1844 when Joseph Taylor, who had joined in 1816, John Fladgate in 1837 and Morgan Yeatman in 1844, all decided to call their partnership that. Their now famous 4XX trademark happily combines tradition with progress.

Taylor's have achieved many 'firsts' in their long history. Perhaps the least sexy, but the most ground-breaking, was the introduction of Late Bottled Vintage port for those who could not afford to wait and finance the mandatory twenty-plus years to enjoy a proper vintage port.

2. FAMILY FAVOURITES

These names are familiar across the generations and, as in all families, contain their own special characters.

COCKBURN

Known as 'singeprick' in the trade, but Cockburn Smithes to give this well-known port house its full and proud name. Robert Cockburn founded his company in 1815. He was later joined by John Smithes in 1848. The legendary John Smithes I met in 1963, with his world class expectoration skills (spitting to you and me), was a direct descendant of his earlier namesake.

Cockburn's were bought by Harveys of Bristol in 1962 and led from the front over many years, but lost their lustre when the company was sold to Beam International. Port does not really thrive corporately. Multinationals, corporations, call them what you will, never seem to quite get the 'passion' call. Their business models have to concentrate on quantity rather than quality. As a result, in the 1970s Cockburn's nearly abandoned its vintage port capabilities, centred on its first-class vineyard in the Upper Douro, Quinta da Tua, to leverage its successful full ruby and Special Reserve qualities. Happily, as my old and learned friend, David Orr, who became MD, said 'the 1983 has to be very good' to get them back into the ratings game. It was and it did, just.

Cockburns has now been bought by the Symington family, so expect to see some much needed TLC applied to this family favourite.

DELAFORCE

The Huguenot Delaforces, sometimes written de la Force, started a port firm in Oporto in 1848. Exactly one hundred years later they sold their well-regarded company to International Distillers and Vintners, IDV, who added it to their existing port portfolio of Croft and Morgan ports. IDV was an excellent multinational, as multinationals go, but when it evolved into Diageo, all the ports went. (Delaforce is now produced by Real Companhia Velha.)

George Delaforce, always affectionately called Wog, was a great character who, upon returning to his office one day, was told that a rather important customer was in occupation. 'I don't care if it is the Duke of Positano, he thundered. 'It is my office. Get him out!'

For many years, David Delaforce championed his cherished brand around the world. David's clear unswerving belief that Delaforce must retain its individuality paid dividends within IDV. David's father, the bookish John Delaforce, who continued to live in Oporto, wrote the seminal book on the Factory House, first published by Christie's in 1979.

Delaforce vintage ports have a style and depth of their own which is provided by their family vineyard Quinta da Corte, near Pinhao. Sometimes understated and often underrated, Delaforce is capable of producing well rounded, fruity and gently luscious vintage ports.

Dow

Dow. As in wow. Dow vintage ports are renowned for their dry, cedar box characteristics. The company can trace its beginnings back to 1798 and has always produced lighter, more feminine wines than some of their peer group. This is mainly defined in the terroir of their prime vineyard, Quinta do Bomfim, which runs alongside the Pinhao bridge over the River Douro.

You will often see the name Dow inscribed on a cartoonist's port label. What excellent product placement, I used to think. I was assured by one of Oliver Preston's predecessors that this was not because at particular cartoonist was necessarily a Dow aficionado, but, simply put, it fitted on the label better than a longer brand name.

For many years, the face of Dow in the UK has been that of Tim Stanley Clarke. Tim's dry wit and long contact list exactly matches the best characteristics of his brand, wonderful dryish 10-, 20- and 30-year-old aged tawny ports which have great length.

Dow is owned by the multi-faceted Symington family, who have done so much to spread the port gospel around the world.

FERREIRA

Ferreira, whose trademark, of course, is an emu, is one of the all too few Portuguese companies who have consistently maintained a solid reputation. It is almost impossible to think of Ferreira

without thinking of Doña Antonia Ferreira's crinoline as she survived the River Douro's treacherous rapids and whirlpools on that fateful day, 12 May 1862. She was a dominant character who produced dominant port wines. Sweeter than most, but always of consistent quality.

Ferreira's main vineyards are now at Quinta da Seixo, with its outstanding hi-tech winery, and at Quinta de Vale de Meao.

The company long benefited from their iconic wine maker, Fernando Nicolau de Almeida. He created the Douro's first great red table wine, *Barco Velha*. I always compare and contrast these rich tempting, long lived wines with those of another iconic wine maker, Serge Hochar, who creates *Chateau Musar* in the Lebanon. Both dangerous terrains, both outstandingly exciting and different wines.

Ferreira is owned by the Guedes family, proprietors of yesteryear favourite, Mateus Rosé, the pink wine that adorned a thousand red-checked bistro tablecloths, and set many of us off on the vinous route.

NOVAL

Noval is famed for many attributes. The name is writ large on their magnificent stone terraces thus providing many touristic photo opportunities. One such stunning terrace has been converted into a swimming pool. They registered the blockbuster 1931 vintage, when practically no one else did: the ultimate recession wine. Noval also produces a tiny amount, measured in hundreds rather than thousands of cases, of Quinta Noval Nacional in declared vintage port years. This rare, and expensive, experience comes from about six thousand ungrafted vines.

The aristocratic van Zeller family owned the company, named after its famous vineyard, Quinta do Noval, for many years, before selling it to the AXA insurance group in 1993. Christian Seely now oversees this port firm, whilst the gentlemanly Cristiano van Zeller is the owner of Quinta Vale Dona Maria.

The real unspoken difference between Noval (the first Portuguese house to sell port, in 1813,) and most of the other port houses, is that its vintage ports, slightly fruitier than most, have always come from their own vineyard in one place. Hence Quinta Noval appears on the label rather than Noval or their original family name, da Silva.

SANDEMAN

The Don – the first iconic logo for a wine. Sandeman was the first port company to advertise their brand in the UK in the 1920s and The Don has since gained worldwide recognition.

I have a theory about Sandeman vintage port. Take a successful port brand, transfer it to your sister company's sherry brand, and in one fell swoop, you destroy the perception of the port brand. This is what Sandeman did and years later, this is what Croft did too. The same 'desynergy'. The trade and consumer both get confused and think the company has lost focus.

Both Sandeman and Croft have historically produced great vintage ports, 1927 and 1963, no less. Their 1963s are certainly undervalued today.

Sandeman was founded in 1790 and claims to have shipped the first vintage port to the UK. The Sandeman family sold out to Seagrams in 1979 but today the company is owned, alongside Ferreira, by the Guedes family. Manuel Guedes kindly showed me his state-of-the-art winery at Quinta de Seixo in May 2008. I think family ownership again will suit The Don.

WARRE

Warre, founded by one John Clark in 1670, is the oldest English port house. (The oldest port house of all, Kopke, founded in 1638, was, rather annoyingly, Dutch.) From 1729 to 1912 there was always a family member based in Oporto. Today the brand is owned by the tentacular Symingtons, but Bill Warre, though in his eighties, is still very much the face of Warre's. Bill's twinkle and *mots justes* are an integral part of any port tasting in London. There is a wonderful direct link, going back centuries, between the past and the present. It is not as though port is produced in Blighty. It is produced in a foreign country with a difficult language and has been for 350 years. Yet it is still the British who control the top companies, invest in future technology and are the guardians of an internationally recognised luxury product. It is the ultimate expat's dream. Hong Kong went back to the Chinese but members of the British community in Oporto are still there, which is a fantastic achievement. They all ought to be designated 'national treasures'.

Warre's now produce a ground-breaking Otima 10-year aged tawny, as well as luscious rich vintage ports, sourced mainly from their top vineyard, Quinta de Cavadinha.

3. PORT LABELS TO WATCH

Here we consider companies which offer that perceived benefit of value for money because they are still relatively undiscovered or which genuinely wish to stay below the parapet.

CHURCHILL

Johnny Graham, a scion of the Graham port family, bravely started his own port company in 1981. He, and his two brothers, called it Churchill Graham, Churchill being his wife's maiden name. But the mighty Symington family did not like Johnny using his/their Graham name. After a cooling-off period, Johnny agreed to call his fledgling company Churchill, dropping the Graham bit. It seems somehow apt that this latest addition to the roll of honour of port companies should carry the same, although unrelated, name as 'the greatest Briton'.

Churchill's main vineyard is Quinta da Gricha and their first vintage port declaration was 1982, not the most prestigious year, but it got them started. Their ports are pleasingly distinctive, especially their 10-year-old white port, pinkish in colour, which is a revelation.

Johnny has an enviable 'nose'. This refers to his uncanny tasting abilities, rather than some freak beak. Like many other port houses, but not the upper crust Taylor's, Churchill's are producing some very interesting Douro red wines.

CROFT

Writing about Croft is rather like writing about your favourite girlfriend. Except I wouldn't know because I have never written about my favourite girlfriend. But you get my gist: it isn't easy.

The good news is that recently she, for Croft is definitely female, has been wooed and won by one Adrian Bridge. Diageo, Croft's former corporate owner, ceded to him any conjugal rights the big beast might once have enjoyed. Adrian, the calm boss, the knight in shining armour (he of the Fladgate Partnership, owners of two of the three Blue Chip ports, Taylor's and Fonseca) has vowed to look after Croft, to nurture her and bring her back to where she belongs in the great port hierarchy. Lucky girl.

Croft Pink is a label watch. So also are Croft's vintage ports. Roeda is their showpiece vineyard, where the fragrant gum cistus, *Cistus ladanifer*, grows. This delightfully aromatic flowering shrub gives Croft ports a luscious lightness that is to be envied.

The Croft family originally came from Yorkshire and the company was founded in 1678. One of Croft's earlier managers was a Mr J. R. Wright. Charles Sellers, the noted nineteenth-century port historian, describes him thus, 'No merchant was more esteemed than Mr Wright. He was a thorough Englishman'.

Go Croft, go...

NIEPOORT

This small, intriguing port house was established in 1842 by Edward Kebe. F. M. van der Niepoort, a Dutchman, joined him five years later. On Kebe's death in 1848, van der Niepoort gained control of this young port shipper. Dirk van der Niepoort is now the fifth generation of Niepoorts to run this individual and outstanding company.

For years, Niepoort aged tawny ports were better known than their vintage ports. Like any non-British firm, they found it difficult to break into the established port market. Buyers all over the world feel more secure, more comfortable with British names.

Fiercely independent, Niepoort constantly strive to improve their vintage port blends, which mainly come from their vineyards Quinta da Napoles and Quinta do Carril, near the River Tedo. These vintage ports are mainly snapped up immediately by the local cognoscenti and thus are quite rare to find.

Their style is one of intense concentrated fruit flavours backed up by excellent tannin structure. As Dirk told James Suckling, 'There are not a lot of old Niepoort vintages left. People just drank them up. They kept their Taylor's and Fonsecas, but thought they should drink their Niepoorts.' An intriguing label for which to keep an eye open.

RAMOS PINTO

The wine trade doth make some queer alliances, on the face of it. Who owns the Portuguese port firm of Ramos Pinto, whose biggest market is Brazil and which is known for its spectacular pre-war art deco advertising? Step forward champagne's ultimate chic brand, Cristal, owner, Louis Roederer.

Adriano Ramos-Pinto, founded in 1880, nearly keeps breaking through the ranks of the British houses, but still has not quite made it. The charismatic Ramos-Pinto Rosas family ceded control to Louis Roederer in 1990. Still housed in a splendid yellow waterfront building dating back to 1708, Ramos Pinto exudes old world courtesy.

Their vintage port style, with good fruit concentration and tannin grip, is derived from two of their five vineyards, Quinta da Bom Retiro, on the River Torto and Quinta da Ervamoira, on the River Coa.

Louis Roederer is not a company to stand still. One day, a bottle of Ramos Pinto could well carry an invisible 'must have' tag on it.

SMITH WOODHOUSE

Charles Symington let me into a secret one day. The Symingtons don't do secrets, so I was ears agog. Then I realised that it was an open secret, so I felt a bit miffed, but not for long. 'Why is it' I asked at a tasting of the full range of Symington ports – and boy do they have a range, Graham's, Dow's, Warre's, Gould Campbell, Vesuvio and so on – 'that in blind tastings I nearly always seem to really enjoy (the lesser known) Smith Woodhouse vintage ports?' He replied, with a smile, 'Because we really enjoy making them and they do not have to come from any particular estate, so we are free to blend according to the year'.

Most of the great labels that we have encountered so far draw their grapes, their raw material, from specific quintas or vineyards. This is practical in order to maintain individual, authentic styles. Follow the same terroir, usually one that you own, and your style will be consistent and recognisable. Other, lesser-known labels like Smith Woodhouse, do not work from a specific terroir or vineyard. They are unfettered by geographical restrictions. Hence it is the ultimate 'winemaker's wine'. The producer crafts it with his chosen blends from sources that may vary vintage to vintage, but his own competitive blending skills will produce a wine that will give the top labels a run for their money: at an enjoyably competitive price, too.

Londoner Christopher Smith, who founded Smith Woodhouse in 1784, was an MP who later became Lord Mayor of London. Doubtless he would be very proud of his vinous legacy.

BROADBENT

Okay, I know Broadbent is not a port shipper as such, but we are talking about port and port people. And anyone who has met Broadbent *pere et fils*, Michael and Bartholomew, cannot possibly object to their inclusion here. Bartholomew lives in the USA and, being entrepreneurial, wanted his own port. Dirk Niepoort has provided the blends from their first vintage, 1994. (A great fan is *Eat, Pray, Love* author Elizabeth Gilbert.)

Bartholomew and I have discussed the obstacles to increasing port consumption in the USA. We agree that the current infatuation of drinkers who prefer 15 and 16 per cent proof California red wines do not feel the need to step up to the wonderful mature virility of port at 20 per cent. It is rather like having two main courses for dinner at 15 or 16 instead of a starter at 12 or 13 and then a main course at 20. To me, 15 or 16 per cent proof table wines can be as about as appealing as alcoholic cough mixture. If I want spirit alcohol I will happily enjoy a whisky or a gin and tonic. I do not want to drill down through a floating surface of alcohol to enjoy my beloved wine. Cut loose, I say, build up your expectations to a magnificent crescendo rather than force immature, grating juice down the hatch throughout your meal.

Michael Broadbent, meanwhile, in *The Great Vintage Wine Book* (1982), has chronicled all port vintages since 1734 'one of the great vintages of the eighteenth century', through 1811 'the famous comet vintage', 1815 'the renowned Waterloo vintage', 1851 'the great exhibition vintage', 1887 'Queen Victoria's Golden Jubilee vintage', 1897 'the Royal Diamond vintage', 1911's the Coronation vintage' to 1977 'the silver jubilee vintage'. One entry I particularly like is Sandeman 1897 'which was fortified with Scotch whisky because all the stocks of (grape) brandy had been used up for the 1896s'. Hurrah, the show must go on!

4. QUINTAS TO VISIT OR TO DRINK

Many are called, but few are chosen. Alphabetically listed, to avoid potential out-of-joint noses. Out-of-joint noses do not make good aroma noses. Let's explore, explore...

QUINTA DO BOMFIM

Turn right over the bridge northwards at Pinhão and after passing some pretty horrendous tank capacity, you are in Dow country. Quinta do Bomfim has been the mainstay of Dow vintage port for generations, nay centuries. Since 1978, in non declared vintage years, you have been able to buy this single quinta port. It is rather like a single vineyard wine. Everyone is doing this now, but it has taken the port producers some time to capitalise on this style of wine. You are getting the production of the best vineyards, mostly in non-vintage port years. Maybe less complex, certainly not needing so long to mature, but the price is right. Bomfim is a perfect example.

Rather like second labels of the great Bordeaux chateaux, single quinta vintage ports are here to stay. What good news for all of us.

QUINTA DA GRICHA

This is Johnny Graham's new venture. The quinta has been producing port since 1840, but only under its own label since the 2000 vintage. Just when I thought the single quinta concept was easy to explain, i.e. that it was produced in non-vintage years, Johnny has decided to produce both his Churchill and his Gricha labels in the same years as vintage declared years.

This is quite clever, because the terroir logic in most classic wine-producing regions is that wine produced from a single terroir area, i.e. a chateau, is more intense than the wine produced from differing terroir areas, i.e. a commune. But the Douro holds not with this logic: shippers' names score more highly than single vineyards. Or do they? Watch this space.

Quinta dos Malvedos

We have now had a 'do', a 'da' and a 'dos'. (We still await a 'de'. Never have worked it out.)

Malvedos is the spiritual home of Graham's rich vintage port. It is also now the proud possessor of three robotic lagares. It is owned by the Symingtons.

For me, it will always be the scene of the great orange throwing contest. Malvedos was the final destination of the moving cricket pitch on board the train from Oporto to Pinhão that I described earlier. The competitive cricketers, led by David Gower and Allan Lamb, simply had to indulge in the 'who can throw the first orange into the River Douro?' game. It always looks so much easier than it is. I don't think Gower's arm has ever really recovered but he is an excellent commentator.

QUINTA DO NOVAL

Noval again breaks the mould as it is the name for their single quinta ports as well as their other blends. The house itself is delightfully kept and its terracing makes it one of the most memorable vineyards in the whole valley. There is even a swimming pool, which has been neatly wedged in between a couple of extremely steep terraces.

I have stood alongside Christian Seely for many an hour when we have both been lashed to our promotional tables at Zachys in New York State. His dedication to Noval is clear for all to see and the fruits of AXA ownership are keenly recognised.

QUINTA DO PANASCAL

This delightful quinta, gently hidden alongside the River Tavora, has been home to Fonseca ports for over one hundred years. Fonseca bought the quinta in the 1970s. Before this time, few British shippers owned the quintas from whom they bought grapes, unless they lived in them, such as at Croft's Roeda or Taylor's Vargellas. By living, I mean for the duration of the harvest plus the odd weekend for the entertaining of overseas customers, preferably British ones of course.

Panascal is happily rustic in its bricks and mortar guise, but if you sample the bottle, you get that wonderful refreshing fullness that characterises all Fonseca ports. Such offerings make it easier for the not so very wealthy to buy and appreciate really good port.

QUINTA DA ROEDA

A classic tea planter's bungalow, up a winding road from Pinhão, which has been sympathetically restored by new owners Taylor's. Stone lagares once again provide 'bespoke' port. Perched high above the (then) awesome rapids of the River Douro, *roeda* means noise in Portuguese. Fortunately the hydro-electric dams of the 1970s have now converted these rushing rapids into lakes of calm. A lone water skier may be seen occasionally, but there is nowhere better to siesta with a glass of chilled aged tawny.

A delightful tradition, when Elsa and Robin Reid were resident hosts, was the waving of handkerchiefs by the hosts and guests alike, as the latter sped away down the drive – full of happy tears both, such was the wonderful hospitality that Roeda always provided.

QUINTA DE VARGELLAS

Not many lairds, whether they be in the Scottish Highlands or the Portuguese highlands, can boast their own railway station, so close and yet so unobtrusive. The contrast between Vargellas, and say, Clapham Junction, says it all.

Vargellas is a most elegant yet friendly 'chateau' as befits a first growth estate, were it based in Bordeaux, and not the Douro. Continuously being restored by Gilly and Alistair Robertson and now often hosted by Adrian and Natasha Bridge, Vargellas has had its fair share of famous, and infamous, guests. Ironically it was bought from Croft in 1893 and today both Croft and Taylor's are under the same ownership. There are sixty-eight hectares of planted vineyards.

Taylor's famous 4XX trademark can be seen at the bottom of the blissfully warm swimming pool.

QUINTA DO VESUVIO

The Duke of Wellington's London house, Apsley House, is still affectionately referred to as Number One, London. This is because it was the first proper London house that you came to from the west. The imposing Quinta do Vesuvio, by a stretch of the imagination, is the first proper quinta in the Douro Valley that you come to from the east. It is huge, covers 325 hectares over seven hills, of which 132 are planted, has its own chapel and eight stone lagares.

The history of the estate spans more than five centuries. It was bought by the Ferreira family in 1823 but Vesuvio is now owned by the Symington clan. Perhaps it should now be called Number One, The Douro.

Vesuvio produces sensational single quinta ports and is poised once again to take its place as a first growth Douro estate.

5. VINTAGE PORTS TO TRY BEFORE YOU DIE.

Well, it is easier and more fun. Why wait?

1927

Port evokes memories of dates more than any other wine. Not every year produces a vintage port. For example, there were no declared vintages in 1925 or 1926 and none in 1928, 1929 or 1930, so 1927 was eagerly seized upon.

By my reckoning, you could choose your bottle from one of thirty-two different port companies. But the vast majority of that vintage have already, not surprisingly, been attacked and downed with relish. The year 1927 did produce possibly the greatest vintage port ever. The year also produced Michael Broadbent MW, certainly the greatest head of Christie's wine sales, ever.

Just to put things in context, it was also the year in which Mae West was sentenced to ten days in jail for obscenity for her play *Sex*; Alfred Hitchcock released his first film *The Pleasure Garden*, Charles Lindbergh became the first man to fly solo non-stop from New York to Paris; and the last of the Model T Ford cars, number 15,007,003, rolled off the assembly line. But much more importantly, the heavens over the Douro Valley were strutting their stuff. They were in the process of shaping the most important constituent part of the vine, namely the grape, into nothing less than perfection. The rest, as they say, is history.

I remember very clearly my first, for I have indeed been fortunate to have more than one, bottle of Taylor's 1927. Nothing had quite prepared me for the wondrous synergy of maturity and fruit. The bouquet took my thoughts to genies and lamps. Other 1927s have since followed, including Croft and Fonseca.

Declared during the great depression of 1929, I am more than a little aware of the potential similarity with the 2007 vintage, declared in the great recession of 2009. Hold on a moment though. Great port is surely more important than mere economics.

1931

This is of course the odd man out. Not only did just six producers declare a 1931 in these most precarious of times, but the jolly butler I told you about pinched a tidy cache, so 1931s really are a rare breed.

In the great wide world, Spain became a republic; the Empire State building was dedicated to the people of New York City; Nevada legalised gambling; Al Capone was convicted of tax evasion and Charlie Parker equalled the cricket record for the earliest date in the county season to reach one hundred wickets.

Noval 1931 is, of course, the ultimate classic if you can find it. But Rebello Valente, the vintage port label of Robertson's (part of Sandeman, then Seagram, now the Guedes family) is a mighty second. The other houses who bravely declared this vintage were Dow, Warre, Burmester and Martinez.

1945

It constantly amazes me that not only did this year signify the end of World War II, but that it also produced amazing vintages in Bordeaux and port. Truly, the good Lord had got it all worked out.

As in most great vintage port years, everyone wants to get on the bandwagon and turn their young two-year-old ruby wines into classic maturing vintage ports. Twenty-eight producers declared this momentous vintage. The thrill of producing such a wonderful wine so soon after peace became a reality must have sent hearts and minds soaring.

What also sent many hearts and minds soaring in 1945 was Humphrey Bogart marrying Lauren Bacall and Juan Peron marrying Evita.

The year 1945 has always been an important investment yardstick, not least because you have the two most important regions historically, Bordeaux and Port, level-pegging on quality. Recently however, demand for first growth Bordeaux chateaux has outstripped that for vintage port. This is clearly illustrated by current values of Lafite and Latour at over £2,000 per bottle ex sales tax and Fonseca and Graham at a mere £1,000 per bottle ex sales tax.

This made me feel better when I gave one of my precious bottles of Croft 1945 to my brother for an important birthday. And yes, he did share it with me: it was in the small print. We enjoyed it hugely, smiling all the while. The fruit is still there, the balance is still there, the enjoyment is still there. And just think how the port world must have sighed with such relief at harvest time: a cause for real celebration.

1963

Fast forward to the swinging sixties – though if you can remember them, 'you probably weren't there' as they say. The Beatles taped ten tracks for their first album including 'Please, please me'. Bob

Dylan released the Freewheeling Bob Dylan album which featured 'Blowin' in the wind'. Alcatraz closed. JFK made his '*Ich bin ein Berliner*' speech before he was so cruelly assassinated later that same year.

The year 1963 provided the first overall outstanding vintage since the aforementioned 1945. Sure, 1947 and 1948 were pretty spectacular. Fonseca 1948 was/is ultra spectacular. Then 1950 and 1955 were charming ladies' vintages and 1960 has lasted longer than most observers would have given it at the time. But somehow, 1963 became a turning point vintage. I have followed this closely over the years. It has slept, opened up, gone a bit dumb, woken up again, taken another leap forward, levelled out, reached another height. Still giving, still fun. Rather like the Beatles music really.

A record number of shippers declared, thirty-five in all. Admittedly, some shippers were less than well known on the vintage port circuit. Krohn, the sherry gurus Gonzalez Byass and Pinto dos Santos being amongst them, but although I am the first to advocate follow the label, not the vintage, in a situation such as the 1963s, everyone should experience this vintage. It has allowed so many consumers to indulge their fantasies and will continue to do so for years to come.

1966

I have included this often underrated vintage because it still tastes so damn good and still gives so much pleasure. So it would be churlish not to, really. It also sorted the sheep from the goats, as it were. Those shippers proud of their young ports declared accordingly, twenty-five of them. Those who were still sitting on their unsold stocks of their 1963s decided to pass on this one. There is no doubt that the 1963 overshadowed the 1966 vintage in most people's minds. But now the 1966s, scarcer to find, are absolutely wonderful to drink.

World events that year included Florence being submerged by floods; the Gemini space programme; Mao's Little Red Book being published in Beijing; the Met Opera House being opened in New York; Cassius Clay beating Henry Cooper in London and John Lennon apologising for saying that the Beatles were more popular than Jesus. It seems another age altogether, which is why it is so fascinating to bridge these years with a bottle of one of the longest lived wines known to man – vintage port.

6. VINTAGES TO DRINK OR CELLAR.

Port has recently fallen out of the 'investment' category, so prices are ridiculously low compared to other great wines of the same age.

1977

This was the vintage that aroused our friends across the pond to appreciate the benefits and enjoyment of vintage port. After the correct 1970 and the changeable 1975, this full, rich vintage ushered in a new era of vintage port drinkers. It was a charismatic year, outstanding in depth, grip and elegant fullness.

Rather like many of those born in the same year, these wines have matured into elegant thirty-plus-year-olds. Confident, not at their peak yet, but their puppy fat has long gone. Some are doing better than others. The best have very attractive personalities that will give much pleasure to their friends in years to come.

Outside the Douro Valley, snow fell in Miami for the first time in living memory; Queen Elizabeth II Silver Jubilee celebrations were watched by an estimated five hundred million people around the world; and Virginia Wade won at Wimbledon.

1994

After the largely best forgotten vintages of the 1980s (although the 1985s are good soft gulpers now) and some releases in 1991 and 1992, it was a huge relief to announce a really great vintage release that would stand and has stood, the test of time.

What separates good vintages from great vintages is largely when the sun shines and the rain rains. If these get out of kilter, the dear little grapes get confused and simply cannot 'fruit up'. You also need a degree of chutzpah. Do I pick the little rascals now or do I wait for that vital ingredient, more sun or more rain? Either could make all the difference between winning or coming second.

That year the Channel Tunnel, employing fifteen thousand workers over seven years, was opened by Mrs Thatcher and M. Mitterrand. Nelson Mandela became South Africa's first black president. A port person, he. Jackie Kennedy Onassis died. Both her husbands were port people. President Nixon died: not a port person. The oldest human ancestor, at 4.4 million years, *Ardipithecus ramidus*, was given that special epithet. He probably missed out on his port.

2003

True to weather and economic conditions, the port shippers stepped neatly back into declaring a vintage port every three years. The years 1997 and 2000 were declared, but it was 2003, with its extraordinarily hot, baking summer that produced the next real winner.

It is a demurely sexy vintage. Try to avoid it under age, but enjoy from 2015 onwards. Resist the fragrant bloom of youth, leave the bottles to get through a dumb adolescence and meet them as confident, still sexy, good-looking adults. Enjoy reminiscing about the summer of 2003 with them.

Other events seem almost recent. The year saw Concorde's last flight. (I well remember eating pheasant at sixty thousand feet on my one Concorde trip to New York in the 1970s. I thought that would be the highest pheasant I had ever got close to, and it was, by miles, British coalition forces launched a war against Iraq, without the authorisation of the UN. Temperatures of over 100 degrees Farenheit were recorded for the first time in the UK. England won the Rugby World Cup in Australia.

2007

All major shippers declared. It is a great vintage, 2007, that will happily outlast the financial crisis. I tasted most in May 2008 and was really impressed that each of the heavyweights – Fonseca, Graham, Warre, Taylor and others – absolutely reflected what one has come to expect from these great port houses.

House styles take their character and balance from their key vineyard sources:
Taylor's, Cockburns, Sandeman have a benchmark mid weight style, with good backbone;
Dow and Croft are on the lighter, sensual side;
Fonseca, Graham and Warre are richer heavyweights.

Beyond the Douro, Paris Hilton, Britney Spears and Lindsay Lohan partied all night; Luciano Pavarotti died and Helen Mirren won an Oscar playing the Queen. A one-hundred-year-old melon was discovered by archaeologists in Japan. *Harry Potter and the Deathly Hallows* was released and sold over eleven million copies in the first twenty-four hours, becoming the fastest selling book in history.

7. POPULAR PORT PAIRINGS

Above all else, drink port with friends; sharing is all. But if you feel like a glass by yourself, go for it. It becomes your friend.

DURING THE DAY

Well, where do you start? Or more cogently, when do you start? Probably not before breakfast, but if you are out shooting on a freezing cold windswept day, then a quick shot of port, with a hot sausage or immediately after one, is very satisfactory and very warming. Better than gloves as it were.

Almost anything is better mid-morning than a perfunctory cup of coffee. Surprise your business host by asking for a glass of chilled 10-year aged tawny port instead. You will be surprised how quickly the ice can be broken and the deal signed.

A hot sunny day demands other tactics. White port is an old craze that has still not really left the Douro Valley. Pink port is the new craze that is fast gathering momentum. Dry white port and tonic, with ice and lemon naturally, accompanied by pan-fried almonds, is the classic port shippers' pairing. This is best taken sitting on a verandah, with friends, in a private quinta in the majestic Douro Valley.

If the invitation got lost in the post, try this pairing at home by the swimming pool. If the swimming pool cannot fit into your apartment, try it on the balcony. If you are a non-dilutionist, enjoy chilled white port with duck pâté or smoked ham.

These pairings encourage conversation, but never pair with a BlackBerry. Emailitis can be very catching. You will lose your train of thought.

Incidentally, pink port, the intriguing creation of Adrian Bridge, is best paired with an attractive young couple. Again, enjoy chilled, and then smile a lot. You have discovered something that others have not.

After lunch, a chilled 10- or 20-year-old tawny port is essential. Delightfully nutty, the entrancing sunset hue will soften the blows of the afternoon. Or you can pair it with a siesta.

DURING THE EVENING

As Alma Cogan and Frank Sinatra so memorably sang in 1956, 'Love and marriage, love and marriage, go together like a horse and carriage ... you can't have one without the other', or words to that effect. They might have included a lyric about 'port and cheese', but they did not, maybe because it wouldn't have rhymed. The classic cheese pairings with port are *queijo de serra* and *marmelada*, aka quince, when in Portugal, and Stilton or Gouda when not in Portugal. For me, a freshly cracked walnut with a smidgeon of sea salt can provide the perfect pairing.

If dinner seems a long way off, you can always take heart from Alfred Lord Tennyson's famous mid-afternoon plea in *Will Waterproof's Lyrical Monologue 1*:

'Oh plump waiter at the Cock
To which I most resort,
"How goes the time?" 'Tis five o'clock.
Go fetch a pint of port.'

Now this may be impinging on tea-time as we know it, but again, what a wonderful way to startle someone in a most elegant way. One can imagine Jeeves complying with such a request with total imperturbability. Crumpets with Gentleman's Relish would seem the most appropriate accompaniment.

After dinner, if you then wish to move up, or down, the self-imposed scale of decadence, a proper cigar provides the perfect pairing opportunity. There is something extremely deep-down satisfying about clasping a glass of rich port in one hand and a fat, lit cigar in the other. A sense of benignness drops the shoulders.

The port hero has two options here. A chilled 10- or 20-year-old tawny contrasts beautifully with the warmth of the cigar. Equally, the warmth of a decanted vintage port complements sumptuously the warmth of the cigar.

No one does decadence better than the port-loving cigar smoker.

8. 'MUST HAVE' PORT ACCESSORIES

A sense of humour helps. Especially when your friends are paying exorbitant sums for their clarets and burgundies and you are having just as much quality fun as you savour your vastly less expensive ports.

A SUFFICIENT CELLAR

Let me try to put this in perspective. The lady of the house tends to get her own way in choosing her ideal kitchen. Whether she uses it much or not, it is to her own specification and probably very much her domaine. Its value probably will not increase, but it looks good in the sale particulars.

The gentleman of the house tends to make do with a wine cellar under the stairs or in an outhouse. He may use this space a lot, but unless there is an underground cellar, it is probably pretty makeshift. Nowadays, the profit from his wine cellar could well pay for two or three bespoke kitchens.

In my view, the time has come, walrus or no walrus, for gentlemen to rise up and demand equal rights. Food and wine require equal billing. There ought to be a law of ratios which stipulates that if a kitchen costs x, then a wine cellar should cost a minimum of y. The gentleman or lady can then spend their well-earned bonuses in laying down a wine cellar to tide them over during the next recession.

This equality has already been achieved, and some would say comfortably surpassed, by several notable wine collectors both in the UK and the USA. These serious temples to the good god Bacchus are to be lauded and applauded.

This preamble also makes a valid point though. A wine and

port cellar, whatever the size, is essential to enjoy good wine and therefore good food. You do not want to rush out and buy bottles off the shelf minutes before you expect guests. Having said that, the easiest quality ports to buy and cellar are the lighter 10, 20 and 30 aged tawny ports and the fuller late bottled vintage ports. The port producer has kindly nurtured and looked after these for us, letting them mature in their ancient oak casks or pipes in the wonderfully vaulted and blackened cellars of Vila Nova de Gaia. He then filters the port before bottling so that the port lies clear, without sediment, in the bottle. A stopper cork is applied. There is no need to lay the bottles carefully on their sides as there is no

gunge in the bottle; no need to let the port mature in bottle as it has been stabilised before bottling. These bottles will taste the same in one or five years time. Just open and pour, and pour, and pour.

Part of the pleasure of sharing interesting wine with friends is the browsing and choosing in your own cellar. This is especially so in the case of vintage port. Vintage port is always special. The names on the labels evoke so many past happy times. To enjoy your vintage ports in the best condition, you want to know where it has been and with whom it has been sleeping over the past ten, twenty or more years. And they all need at least ten and preferably more than twenty years for these young things to mature properly. If the vintage port has been stored next to a radiator or been tossed and turned too vigorously, thus deprived of the horizontal sleep that every good vintage port needs, then she will turn out to be a bad muddled girl. If the vintage port has been kept in one cellar at a constant temperature, then she will present herself impeccably.

The reason for all this fuss is that, by definition, vintage port is bottled unfiltered and unstabilised, so it does change character significantly when lying on its back for all these years. Wouldn't you?

I have seen perfectly capable captains of industry get into a complete tizz about their vintage port. They go all wobbly at the knees at the worry of 'not doing it right'. Forget the day job, this is what really counts.

Treat these historic pitfalls of tradition as modern fine wines. Open, decant, pour and enjoy, but in a large port or white wine glass. A red wine glass if naught else is available. Simply tack them on the end of your last red wine: and enjoy.

HERE ARE SOME DO'S AND DON'TS.

DO lay down your vintage port with the label or white paint dash facing upwards. This allows the sediment or gunge to discard equally to the opposite side. Move infrequently, if at all, until you wish to drink.

DO keep a constant temperature between 8°C and 12°C and humidity at 70 per cent. A higher humidity may cause the labels to disintegrate. If labels have disintegrated, the shipper's name and vintage will be on the cork.

When you have selected your vintage port for the evening, **DO** stand it up for twenty-four hours. This will enable the sediment to congregate in the punt in the bottom of the bottle.

DO decant into a decanter straightaway or double decant into a jug first, then dry the empty bottle and pour the port back into it. Unlike many great red wines, vintage ports will always, always have sediment, because they are bottled unfiltered. The sediment does no harm. It just looks murky.

DON'T worry about the infernal wax. Just get it off.

DON'T worry about the cork disintegrating. Just jam it down, carefully. But if you are looking for the shipper and/or the vintage, enjoy the jigsaw puzzle.

DON'T worry about candles or muslin. Just hold the bottle steady until you see things that you should not see. When this happens, you will note that most of the remaining wine is cradled in the shoulder. Practice makes perfect.

DON'T worry about 'bottle stink'. Old wine which has been locked up for twenty, thirty or more years needs space to stretch, to evolve. Imagine if you had been locked up, as it were, for this length of time, you might smell a tad and would need a Sunday walk at least. This odour will disappear after a few minutes. Too many fine old bottles of delicious wine have been jettisoned by impatient owners who do not wait for this natural occurrence.

DON'T ever, ever ask your guests if they would like vintage port. Just serve it. Lead from the front. Then your Croft 1970, Gould Campbell 1977 or Taylor's 1985 becomes a normal quality red wine rather than some special untouchable danger zone. A well-produced and well-matured port of 20 per cent alcohol will have much less effect the morning after than an immature red wine of 15 per cent alcohol, and have given you so much more pleasure. You want more rather than less.

DECANTERS AND GLASSES

Port decanters have many uses. You can never have too many of them. Empty ones make an elegant display and enhance any dining room. Full ones, rather like magnums, signify that your host cares and that you are about to enjoy a party.

Decanters come in all shapes and sizes. Most port decanters have round flat bottoms; the Bishop of Norwich decanter, formally called the Hoggett, has a round, round bottom. This means it can never be placed on the table, otherwise it will fall over. It has to be passed to your neighbour. That would have sorted the Bish. But it can also make the host, who keeps its rounded coaster near him, sometimes be a little bit Bish-like himself.

Bruce Guimaraens, the late and much-lamented partner of Fonseca Guimaraens, once asked a neighbour at dinner if he 'knew the Bishop of Norwich'. 'Why yes', replied the innocent, 'why do you ask? He is my father-in-law.' Bruce was left fuming at the out of reach decanter. He could not, would not, bring himself to enlighten the younger man as to the real meaning of his question.

Now let's consider glasses, a delicate subject. On the one hand, the unsuspecting, and frankly uninitiated, will happily consume port out of a small port glass. Those ghastly elgin glasses are still around. But small glasses simply do not allow a natural appreciation of fine wine. Enter 'Smasher' Robertson. (He, the elegant chairman of one of the greatest port names, Taylor's.) 'No one would ever serve Château Petrus or Château Lafite in a tiny little glass, so why serve a 20-year-old tawny or a 1977 vintage port in a vessel that mutes rather than flatters the wine's qualities?' he once demanded. 'Smasher' once confided in me with a glint in his eye, 'I usually use an empty magnum to ensure that the tiny glass is definitely dead.'

Whilst sitting on the Royal Household Wine Committee, which

'SMASHER' ROBERTSON

I did for twenty-one years, I think my most valuable contribution was to help persuade the Monarch to offer larger port glasses to her guests. At first sight, this may seem a small contribution in the overall scheme of things. Upon reflection, just think how much more animated a conversation per glass can now be achieved at state banquets.

The Royal family, in general, are not port people in the nicest possible way, but the Royal Cellars do contain some excellent vintages as you would expect. The only trouble was that these wonderful vintage ports used to be served in thimble-sized port glasses. The vintage ports must have felt so frustrated. They had been preparing themselves for decades, then suddenly whoosh, and straight down the gullet. No gentle swaying or swirling, no admiration, no sniffing, no nothing. They didn't have a chance to show themselves off. Great port should be enjoyed as a great wine, not out of a thimble.

DRESS CODE

Anything – fez, jeans, sweater, smoking jacket – apart from a suit. Obviously a dinner jacket, or white tie, is fine for formal occasions, but never a suit.

A suit indicates that you have either had a busy day at the office and need a good night's sleep or that you are doing something tomorrow, usually terribly important, such as a power breakfast, or catching the (often mythical) early morning flight. Yawn. Either way, you will looked pained when the port is offered or passed. And refuse it. Yawn.

Never a suit.

9. PORT SPORTS

Tiddlywinks may qualify, kick-boxing probably not. Sailing naturally does, especially if you are relaxing on the port side; roller-skating probably doesn't.

CRICKET

It has been wisely said that 'those exercises which... have a direct tendency to draw the bands of society closer together in friendly intercourse, and which are free from the taint of selfishness... are entitled to special encouragement. There is no field exercise in vogue which so fully answers the above... as cricket. The pluck, nerve and courage of true manhood are the essential characteristics of cricket.'

For over one hundred years, the regular influx of cricket teams to Oporto has provided the lifeblood of the port shippers' social and sporting life. Representatives of the UK wine trade visit twice a year, thus cementing vital trade relationships which cannot be achieved in an office. Imagine bowling your best customer for a duck or hitting a six off your pet-hate customer.

The Lords and Commoners, the Law Society and the Free Foresters teams all covet their annual Portuguese visits, not least because the lunch in the Pavilion is always followed by one or two or three glasses of chilled old tawny port. An inordinate amount is usually consumed, but play always resumes and afterwards there is always time to contemplate, time to discuss, time to enjoy. Cricketers are natural and naturally port people.

FOOTBALL

Rugby football is a classic port sport. Rugby players tend to be jovial, generous people with an inbuilt sense of humour. They give their all when on the pitch and give their all when off the pitch. 'Rugger buggers' play hard and work hard. They are successful team players and successful life players. Tankards would probably be their preferred port drinking vessels.

Football, or soccer, on the other hand, is difficult to characterise. Is it a port sport or a game dominated by too much money, too many foreigners and not enough fun? A beautiful game or a business? Maybe some box-holders are port people but most players are not? The jury is out.

HUNTIN', SHOOTIN', FISHIN'

These classic outdoor activities attract classic outdoor personalities from all social strata. This is England, or Great Britain, or the United Kingdom (which are we?) at its best.

Field sports often define a country. We are proud of ours. I will ignore the pernicious 2004 Hunting Act, but will raise a glass of port to all those who respect their quarry, be they foxes, game birds or fish.

A glass of port at the meet is so traditional that even the foxes would feel something was awry if this hunting ceremony stopped. Similarly, if bottles of port were missing from the mid-morning hamper after the second or third drive during a day's shooting, it might be the keeper that was shot rather than the birds.

Port keeps you warm amongst kindred spirits. There is more 'going on' in port than in most spirits, even kindred ones. The exception to this rule is sloe gin, the only drink that amateurs can make better than the professionals. Drinks at sporting events encourage banter and banter is inherently healthy.

Few sports offer a day better suited for getting to know your fellow guests really well than shooting. At the pre-shoot dinner, if the claret is excellent, then as the vintage port should be older, the clue is that you are heading into a magnificent day's shooting. The next morning, when choosing one's peg, I have known the numbers to be concealed underneath glasses of port, so that is the first one of the day down the hatch.

Then come mid-morning refreshments. Sloegasms for the prudent; sloe gin for those whose wails of 'bang, bang, bugger, bugger' can be heard up and down the line; port for those whose ratio is almost inverse.

At luncheon, a 10-year-old tawny port raises expectations for the afternoon's sport.

At tea-time? No thanks, I really am driving...

'Real men drink port... and Ladies do too.' There can be few more welcome and beautiful infiltrators into the 'real men...' lifestyle than the Covert Girls, an offshoot of the Shooting Society, whose five rules include 'poaching each other's birds mercilessly, but never one's men' and 'all loaders must be male, hot and know how to dress in white tie'. After this 'Lipstick, powder and Purdey' article appeared in *The Field*, I immediately called the Covert Girls founder, Claire Zambuni, to ask whether she and her fellow shots enjoyed port. 'Of course we do. We enjoy everything and adore men!' she exclaimed. She had even recently had to resort to fetching a bottle of port from her car as the hotel where they were staying had run out. Now that is class. These dashing ladies will happily shoot in the rain rather than shop in the rain, and port is very much part of their sport; these ladies certainly do not leave the table after dinner.

A kind of new world order has taken over from the times when 'men Ranged and girls Sloaned'. We are all in it together now and much the healthier for it.

SKIING

The first gentle swoosh. Adrenaline. The perilous cable car hitched to a far off snowy peak. *Where Eagles Dare?* Adrenaline. Downhill only. Adrenaline.

Lunch: banter.

Last Black run of the day. Adrenaline.

Dinner: banter.

After dinner. With all this adrenaline and banter, relationships develop at twice or three times the normal pace. There is probably no time for port before bedtime. But back home, at normal speed, these same gregarious, attractive, sporty, smiley men and women will doubtless make time for a glass of port before bedtime…

10. CONTEMPORARY PORT HEROES

This is where you and I come in. You don't have to have climbed Everest or swum the Pacific, you just have to enjoy one of the world's most spoiling drinks. Easy really! My heroes include:

The port producers and shippers themselves. These are the selfless heroes whose day job it is to sniff and taste, sniff and taste. Then they have to entertain, have to entertain. It is a very closed shop and a much coveted lifestyle. At the risk of a serious omission, I will name and shame the leaders of this extraordinarily successful tight-knit pack who mainly provide for the quality port markets. Without them, port enthusiasts all over the world would go seriously dry. Let us salute: Generations of Symingtons – Michael, James and Ian; Paul, Dominic, Johnny, Charles, Clare and Rupert Symington; Bill Warre. The Fladgate Partnership: Alistair Robertson, Huyshe Bower, Adrian Bridge, Natasha Robertson, Robert Bower. The late Bruce Guimaraens. Other port characters, in no particular pecking order, including Johnny Graham, Robin Reid, Christian Seely, Dirk Niepoort, Christiano van Zeller, Nick Heath, Peter Cobb, Tim and Sophia Berqvuist.

Godfathers, who have, over many generations, selflessly given their godsons, and now goddaughters, vintage port from their birth, or conception year. Originally a pipe, 60 dozen or 720 bottles, would be laid down for this lucky wee chap to indulge in once he had reached twenty-one. Now it is likely to be a case, one dozen or 12 bottles. The age-old rationale is of course two fold. Vintage port tends to mature at twenty-one years; also the godfather has every intention of sharing this investment with his godson. Which has fared better ?

Port wives. Those who entertain previously unknown business customers, those who are evacuated from the dining room before due time, those who welcome their men back late at night after 'just one more glass'. Those of you, and I am thinking of one delightful Northamptonshire lady in particular, who left her then husband to his 'dreaded port' at a friend's dinner party and drove home by herself. You know who you all are. Take a well-deserved bow.

Wine courses, such as the WSET, Christie's, Berry Brothers, Waddesdon and Michael Schuster who act as the go-between twixt the producer and the enthusiast.

Oxford and Cambridge colleges, where a lifetime's serious port drinking has begun for many serious wine lovers, over many centuries. College cellars are amongst the finest in the world. The richer the college, probably the older the port.

Livery companies, where layers upon layers of binned port have slumbered in the City's underground cellars over many centuries, until happily awakened for a dinner and enjoyed with the loyal toast.

St James's Clubs, where port drinking has been a ritual for several centuries, until the dastardly smoking ban which has somewhat curtailed consumption. 'Two glasses of Club vintage port, please' is one of the most welcome cries a guest can ever hear.

Historic wine dining clubs, such as Northamptonshire's Aquitaine, where two vintage ports are always tasted blind or The Cellarmans at the Savile Club, where members bring their own, often ancient, bottles to be objectively assessed by their friends.

Last, but certainly not least, Roy Hersh's website www.fortheloveofport.com is a continually inspiring conduit for those who are proud to be 'port heads' instead of, or as well as, 'petrol heads'. 'Port heads' that I have spoken to, in the US or the UK, love the idea of taking ancient bottles of vintage ports back to Oporto or the Douro to share these historic treasures with those whose ancestors produced the wine on the selfsame spot. Taking petrol back to the oil-field does not have quite the same appeal. Roy told me the delightful story of a port tasting in Seattle in 2003 attended by Christies legendary Michael Broadbent. Apparently, Michael was tasting the equally legendary Noval Nacional 1931. After some time, for no particular reason, Michael pronounced that this was the regular Noval vintage blend, not the fabled Nacional. No reasons were given; no questions were asked. As Roy said, that was his lore.

And finally, **Sir Ranulph Fiennes**, an old flat-mate of mine and the world's greatest living explorer, who actually has climbed Everest. He confided to me that at Eton during Army Cadet Force outings, older boys used to commission Ran and several others in his 'smuggling group', including Jeremy Deedes, son of the legendary Bill Deedes, to visit the nearest Victoria Wine shop to buy port for them. Ran's commission was 2/6d (old money, 12½p new) per bottle. He then smuggled said bottles over Windsor Bridge in the pockets of his tailcoat.

Other celebrity port enthusiasts, including:
Claudia Schiffer
Mick Jagger
Gary Lineker
Peter Stringfellow
Cliff Richard
David Beckham
David Gower
Father Christmas
(leave blank – add your name here)

11. PORT POLITICIANS

Recent and contemporary, my choices are limited to those of British and American nationality.

SIR WINSTON CHURCHILL

The greatest Briton enjoyed Dow's 1896 in the trenches during the Great War. Maurice Symington's great-grandson, Rupert, told me that they had somehow managed to get the port through the lines. Churchill and Symington shared this great vintage, doubtless with fellow officers. When they met after the war, Churchill greeted his war-time friend by prodding his stick at him, exclaiming 'Port, port!'. Although, in later years, Churchill's penchant for champagne and cognac is well documented, he must be included if only for his indomitable bulldog grit and wit: very port characteristics.

BARONESS THATCHER

Denis, the greatest husband, certainly enjoyed his port. He would have had time for many conversations both on and off the golf course, where liquid fortification would have been welcome. I suspect the formidable Maggie would also have enjoyed her port had someone told her you could chill it. Instead she was a patriotic whisky enthusiast.

Political son of Thatcher, John Major, holidayed twice in the Douro. So he qualifies, not least because of his visit to The Oval after he was 'let go' and because of his courteous and gentlemanly charm.

Carol a port person; Mark not a port person.

TONY BLAIR AND GORDON BROWN

Tony is the archetypal non port person. As his old college porter at St John's Oxford, who retired in 2011, remembered him, 'He was a long haired git who played the guitar'. Then he grew up. He wanted to change everything without thinking things through. He would obviously want to pass the port to the right, except, no that cannot be right, too controversial; he would then look to the left, no that is going backwards; he would then deftly try to find a third way, that might work, then he would panic, reach for his mobile and call Alastair Campbell.

Gordon would probably knock the port glass over by stretching to the left, then pick it up and throw it at someone perhaps.

RONALD REAGAN AND BILL CLINTON

Ronald Reagan seemed to make time to talk, to be genial and self-deprecating. He once could not find out how to switch the television on in his bedroom when staying at a house in Battersea. A giggly girlfriend of ours, who had been helping out with the flowers, was detailed to explain to him, alone, way past midnight that he had not actually switched the plug on at the wall. 'God darn it,' Reagan told her. 'You wouldn't believe that I have been President of the United States, not only once, but twice'. A port person indeed.

Bill Clinton, on the other hand, apparently could not wait for dinners to be over at the White House. Daniel Shanks, head of the Ushers' Office who organised these events, told me that forty-five minutes was his ideal length of time. Probably not a port person, then.

DAVID CAMERON AND BORIS JOHNSON

The Prime Minister and the London Mayor must have enjoyed port together during their Bullingdon days at Oxford. The fact that they both enjoyed a private education by going to a public school, so confusing for anyone who lives outside our great country, would indicate that they got stuck in once or twice.

Cameron appears to be thoughtful and to lead at his own speed. Johnson appears to be witty and lead at his own speed. Givers not takers: port people, both.

The common factor with port people is the ability to look someone in the eye and above all, to smile with your eyes.

To sum up, an enthusiasm for port reflected the aspirations of bulldog Englishmen during the reigns of several Georges and a Victoria. This species now seems to be out of favour with mainstream Britishness and so does port. This is disheartening for those, who, like Ranulph Fiennes, have shown leadership at its most humble, yet are so admired across the globe. We cannot all achieve in such a gallant way, but it is never too late to try. Of course, most of our days are taken up with such vinous delights as champagne, manzanilla, burgundy, bordeaux wines from Chile and New Zealand and tokaji as well as port.

Port may not have been the first wine to have encroached upon the Englishman's soul, but, by golly, history has shown that a port person has the right attitude to life. 'Port people of today' have so much to offer.

A glass is always more attractive if it is half full, rather than half empty. A port person will aspire to ensuring that his or her glass is always more than half full. Hosts beware – but then hosts are themselves port people.

BIBLIOGRAPHY

Barr, Ann and York, Peter *The Official Sloane Ranger Handbook,* Harpers & Queen 1982

Bespaloff, Alexis *The Fireside Book of Wine,* Simon & Schuster 1977

Bradford, Sarah *The Story of Port,* Christie's Wine Publications 1978

Broadbent, Michael *The Great Vintage Wine Book,* Mitchell Beazley 1980

Burke, Thomas *English Night Life,* Batsford 1943

Cobb, Gerald *Oporto Older and Newer,* 1965

Delaforce, John *The Factory House of Oporto,* Christie's Wine Publications 1979

Fletcher, Wyndham *Port,* Sotheby Park Bernet 1978

Howkins, Ben *Rich Rare & Red,* Wine Appreciation Guild 3rd Edition 2003

Johnson, Hugh *Wine: A Life Uncorked*, Weidenfeld & Nicolson 2005

Knox, Oliver *Croft, A Journey of Confidence*, Collins 1978

Nimrod *The Life of John Mytton*, Methuen 1949

O'Brien, Donough and Welden, Anthony *Numeroids*, Bene Factum 2008

Robertson, George *Port*, Faber & Faber 1978

Robinson, Jancis *Confessions of a Wine Lover*, Penguin 1997

Searle, Ronald *Wine Speak*, Souvenir 1983

Suckling, James *Vintage Port*, Wine Spectator Press 1990

Symington, James *A Life in the Port Trade*, 2007

Todd, William *Port*, Jonathan Cape 1926

Warre, William *Letters from the Peninsula 1808-1812*, Spellmount 1999

Waugh, Alec *Merchants of Wine*, Cassell and Company 1957

Wheatley, Dennis *The Eight Ages of Justerini's 1749-1965*, Dolphin 1965

INDEX